Home-made Christmas

with 35 beautiful easy-to-make projects

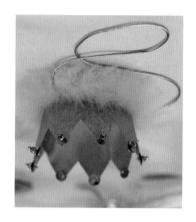

Tessa Evelegh

photography by Caroline Arber

CICO BOOKS

LONDON NEW YORK

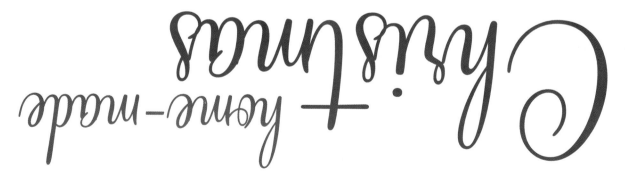

Published in 2009 by CICO Books
An imprint of Ryland Peters & Small Ltd

20–21 Jockey's Fields   519 Broadway, 5th Floor
London WC1R 4BW   New York, NY 10012

www.cicobooks.com

10 9 8 7 6 5 4 3 2 1

Text © Tessa Evelegh 2009
Design and photography © CICO Books 2009

A CIP catalog record for this book is available from the Library
of Congress and the British Library.

ISBN-13: 978 1 906525 82 8

Printed in China

Editor: Pete Jorgensen
Designer: Luis Peral-Aranda
Photographer: Caroline Arber

*In memory of my mother, Ann Evelegh, who
always made Christmas so special, but
who made this one her last.*

Contents

introduction

Bringing out the decorations, putting up the tree, and decking the house always bring a seasonal frisson. Christmas is here! And nestling, hidden somewhere in the corner of a box or bottom of a bag, is some forgotten favorite that revives memories of Christmases past. Commercial excess, which increasingly dominates this special holiday, recedes as the family gets together to trim the tree, make delicious treats, and decorate the home.

Traditionally, decorations were always handmade using materials that could be found around the house and gleaned from nature. It's still immensely satisfying to make your own—children love to help, and making ornaments and gifts is a wonderful way to fill the days of anticipation. Every year our family has a Christmas decoration-making afternoon. Friends and family get together to stick, thread, bind, and sequin all kinds of decorations, which have built up over the years to create a richer and richer tree. Even with a year between each session, our tree has developed a surprisingly cohesive look. The key is to stick to an overall color scheme. Ours is silver, gold, pink, purple, and red, so each year, when planning what to make, we surround ourselves with lots of materials within our color range.

Bringing this experience to bear, you'll find most of the projects in this book require only the most basic of skill level, so even the most obstinate "I'm-just-not-the-creative-type" can have a go with guaranteed success! The joy of Christmas decorations is that they're not meant to be masterpieces. They're fun; they're quick; they can even be kitsch. But en masse, they're always beautiful. This book has over 35 projects and ideas to get you started. Use them, adapt them, develop your own, because when it comes down to it, the best part of homemade is that it's an expression of yourself.

seasonal welcome

Christmas is all about welcome! It's the time of year when many workplaces shut down for a few days, giving us time to concentrate on family, friends, and neighbors and to open our homes for fun and festivities. Start the welcome before they even step over the threshold by decorating the door, putting festive lights in the windows, even hanging a kissing bough in the porch. And whatever your decorations, they'll bring festive cheer to the streets, brightening the long nights, even for passers by.

pine and cinnamon wreath

Nostalgia is a key part of Christmas: the annual thrill of dusting down the decorations; the distinctive aroma of pine and cinnamon, and, when it comes to it, the ham or the turkey and all the trimmings. When asked, most people say they love their Christmas to be traditional with a twist—and that's the appeal of this wreath. All the basics are there—the pine and cones, the cinnamon and oranges, each element harking back to Christmases past—but the feather-like pink foliage adds a lively contemporary touch to make it just that little bit different.

Materials

- 1 pack dried orange slices
- 1 pack dried apple slices
- 20-gauge florist's wire or fine-gauge garden wire
- 5 bundles of raffia-tied cinnamon sticks
- 15 pine cones
- 10in (25cm) fresh pine wreath (finished size 14in/36cm)
- Selection of pink foliage
- Wire cutters
- Pruning shears

1 Start by preparing the material: the dried orange and apple slices should be bundled into groups of three or slices of a similar size. Pass some florist's wire through the bundle and twist the ends together. The cinnamon bundles should be wired through the raffia ties.

2 For the pine cones, pass a wire around the base, wind between the open 'leaves,' and twist the ends together. Bundle the cones into groups of three and twist the wire ends together. Wire the cone bundles to the wreath at equal intervals by pushing the wires right through the pine to the underside of the wreath.

3 Next, wire the apple slices and cinnamon bundles next to the cones, then fix on the orange slices. Make sure they are spaced evenly for a pleasing overall effect.

4 Finally, fix in the pink foliage all around the wreath at an angle pointing outward. This not only creates a more pleasing, dynamic look, but also firmly fixes the foliage. Trim any untidy areas with pruning shears if necessary.

pussy willow wreath

At their best, wreaths cheer the streets on the darkest of days, revealing just a little about the house and family behind the door. But most of the traditional materials—pine, holly, ivy, and cones—are naturally dark, and virtually disappear as the sun goes down, meaning that beautiful wreaths are often overlooked by passers-by. Here, pussy willow and white-sprayed cones lighten up traditional foliage, whilst downy white swans' feathers lend an irresistibly tactile softness to the wreath. Look for the feathers in the milliners' section of a haberdashery or sewing store, where they often come in ready-wired bunches.

Materials

- 8 pussy willow stems
- Pruning shears
- Wire cutters
- Reel florist's wire or fine-gauge garden wire
- 5 fir cones, lightly sprayed white
- 10in (25cm) fresh fir wreath (finished size 14in/36cm)
- 6 white milliner's feathers
- 1yd (1m) white organza ribbon

1 Start by cutting pussy willow stems into 10in (25cm) lengths with pruning shears. Next, cut lengths of wire about 12in (30cm) long and wire up the base of each stem and each cone. For the pussy willow, bend the wire in half and place it about 2in (5cm) up the stem. Wind both ends down to the end of the stem, then twist together. For the cones, just tuck the middle of the wire around the lowest part of the cone, then wind around tightly and twist the ends together.

2 Attach the pussy willow stems to the wreath at an angle. Take your cue from the direction in which the fir has been fixed onto the wreath. Poke the wire right through the base and bend it underneath to fix firmly.

3 In the same way, fix the cones and the feathers. Milliner's feathers are ideal because they come ready-wired in bunches. However, if you can't source them, wire up white feathers in bunches of three in a similar way to the pussy willow stems.

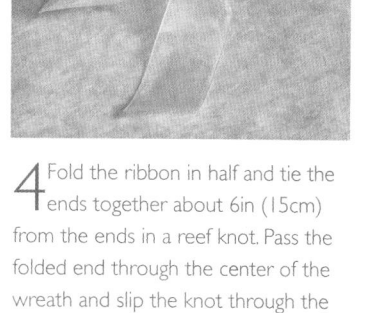

4 Fold the ribbon in half and tie the ends together about 6in (15cm) from the ends in a reef knot. Pass the folded end through the center of the wreath and slip the knot through the loop. Pull tight to create a hanging loop.

kissing bough

Pretty and witty, a generous kissing bough hung above the doorway brings a sense of fun to seasonal greetings. Kissing under the mistletoe is an ancient winter solstice tradition, rooted in Norse mythology and the Druids' belief that the plant had magical powers. And although early Christians condemned it as pagan, they nevertheless embraced the custom under the guise of a holy kiss of peace and pardon. More romantically, legend has it that a woman would be married by the end of the year if she was kissed under the mistletoe. Holly berries were often added to kissing boughs to fill them out and introduce color. Here, holly twigs are complemented by gingham ribbon in berry red.

Materials

- 20 stems mistletoe
- 5 branches ilex (holly berries)
- Florist's stub wires or fine-gauge garden wire
- Wire cutters
- 4½yd (4.25m) wire-edge gingham ribbon, 1½in (3.5cm) wide
- 16in (40cm) willow wreath
- Bucket
- 5ft (1.5m) variegated trailing ivy

1 Prepare the mistletoe and ilex branches by winding wire around the end of each stem. Wind the wire above and below the bottom branching stem to secure it firmly in place.

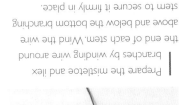

2 Cut the gingham ribbon into four equal lengths. Tie the end of one piece onto the wreath, leaving the rest of the length free to use later in step 5. Repeat with the other three pieces, ensuring they are placed an equal distance apart. Trim the ends of the ribbons diagonally.

3 Rest the wreath on an upturned bucket. Push the wire of one ilex branch into the top surface of the wreath and pass it through to the underside to fix. Let the branch hang downwards. Repeat with the other ilex branches, spacing them equally.

5 Twine the ivy around the willow wreath to cover up the wires. Gather up the ribbons and knot them together about 10in (25cm) from the ends. Make sure they are all tied at the same point above the wreath to ensure it hangs straight. Make another knot a little above the first and hang up, arranging the top to make a pleasing bow. Once the kissing bough has been hung up, add in extra foliage if needed.

4 In the same way, attach the mistletoe to the wreath, spacing it evenly between the ilex branches. Once you have positioned all the branches, you should have a generous "skirt" of the mistletoe and ilex.

cranberry heart

The rich seasonal hues of cranberries make them the ideal material for making Christmas decorations. They stay firm for a week or more, then gradually dry out and develop an even richer red color, which means they will easily outlast the festive season. Here, they have been used to make a delightful heart, which has been whipped around with raffia and can be decorated with a miniature lantern. The finished piece can be used as a door wreath, hung at the window, or used as a decoration indoors. Make several if you have time, one for each downstairs window to make a heartfelt welcome.

Materials

- 2¹/₂yd (2m) heavy-gauge garden wire
- Wire cutters
- Pliers
- 1 pack cranberries—10oz (300g) is plenty
- Raffia
- 20in (50cm) fine-gauge silver-plated wire
- 1 small glass jar
- Sticky tape
- Organza ribbon
- 1 tea light

1 Cut the wire into two equal lengths with wire cutters and make a loop at one end of each piece using the pliers. Thread cranberries like beads onto one wire and make a hook at the other end. Bend the cranberry 'necklace' into a circle and connect the two ends to form a loop, then close the hook. Repeat with the second piece of wire.

2 Bring the two cranberry circles together with the hooked points next to each other. Taking three lengths of raffia, bind the circles together, starting at the point where the ends of the wires are hooked in place.

3 When you get to the end of the raffia, tie in another three lengths and continue binding. At the end of the circle, tie the pieces of raffia together.

4 Now bend the circles into a heart shape with the wire joins at the bottom point. Using six lengths of raffia, tie a generous knot over the exposed wire hooks at the bottom of the heart, then trim to neaten.

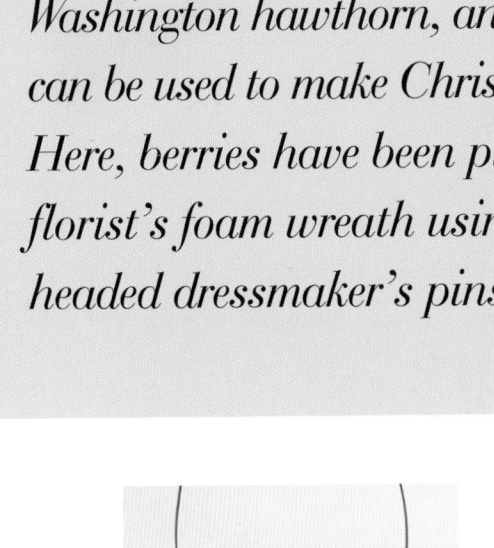

Any firm red winter berries, such as holly, Washington hawthorn, and some euonymus, can be used to make Christmas decorations. Here, berries have been pinned into a florist's foam wreath using white glass-headed dressmaker's pins.

5 First, make a wire band around the top of the jar with a small 'eye' either side to hook the handle to. This will keep the handle firmly in place and help to avoid a fire risk. To do this, cut a length of silver wire about 1½ times the length of the circumference of the glass jar. Fold it in half and make an 'eye' (see step 1 page 44). Pass the two ends around the top of the jar to the point opposite the first 'eye.' Twist them together so the wire is firmly fixed around the top of the jar. Make a second 'eye' at this point so that it is exactly opposite the first 'eye' and just twist the spare ends back around the band.

6 Using the pliers, make a hook at each end of the remaining length of wire and attach to the 'eyes.' Close the hooks so the 'handle' is firm.

7 Tie a piece of raffia around the rim of the jar to hide the wire. Tape the length of organza ribbon around the jar, then tie some raffia around this.

8 Take three lengths of raffia and fold them in half to find the middle. Knot this under the top dip of the heart and the handle of the lantern, so that the candle will hang securely in the center of the heart. Tie the ends of the raffia together at the top and use this to hang up the heart.

A Yuletide Scene

When planning Christmas decorations, think of the space as a whole, and choose a theme that can encompass the tree, stairways, fireplaces, surfaces, and even ceilings. Create impact by carrying the theme through from the front door, right through to the hall and living area, transforming your home into a winter wonderland to light up the darkest of seasons. This hall has been given a simple country woodland feel that is rooted in Scandinavian tradition with a light, contemporary feel. A base of lichen twigs and pine has been lifted by white-sprayed and sparkly twigs for a fantasy frosted feel. Bunting made from triangles cut from green and red printed cottons brings color to the country feel. The whole scene has been liberally seasoned with lanterns, candles, and fairy lights, bringing a Scandinavian influence.

light heart

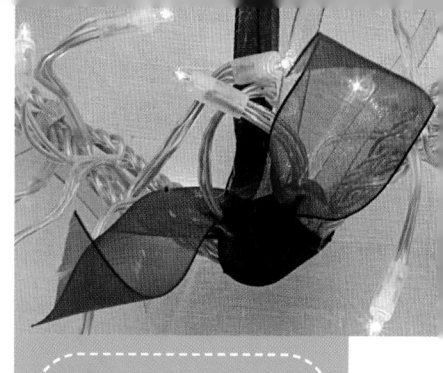
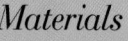

Hang a heart of lights in the window to brighten the dark days of winter. It's a heartfelt message to passers-by and one that can linger on long after Christmas until the days begin to lengthen into springtime. Easy to make, it consists of a lighting chain simply tied to a wire hanger bent into a heart shape, then decorated with gauzy ribbon. Light, bright, and pretty, this heart brings joy wherever it hangs. Add to the impact by making one for each window.

Materials

- Wire cutters or heavy-duty scissors
- 1 wire coat hanger
- Pliers
- 3yd (3m) pale pink organza ribbon, ¼in (0.5cm) wide
- 3yd (3m) claret organza ribbon, 1½in (3.5cm) wide
- Lighting chain at least 10ft (3m) long

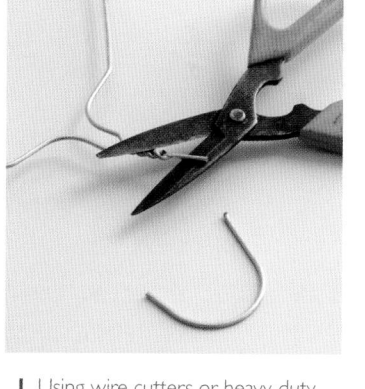

1 Using wire cutters or heavy-duty scissors, cut the hook off the wire coat hanger and bend it into a heart shape with pliers. Next, cut the narrow pink ribbon into 5in (12cm) lengths and the wider claret ribbon into 7in (18cm) lengths.

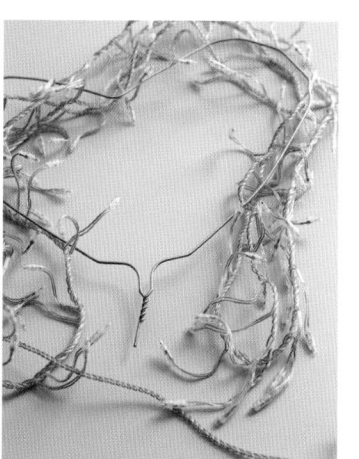

2 Leaving enough excess wire to plug the lights in at the wall, fold the lighting chain into three. Fold this in half to mark the center. Place this center at the dip in the wire heart and use a short piece of ribbon to tie the lighting chain to the hanger.

3 Using the fine pink ribbon pieces, continue tying the lighting chain to the wire heart. It is easiest to start from either side of the dip and then work down both sides of the heart, tying at intervals until you reach the bottom.

4 Tie lengths of the claret-colored ribbon to the center top, the bottom, at the widest points of the heart, and further down the sides. Make the hanging tie by folding the remainder of the claret ribbon in half and tying it together 6in (15cm) from the end.

 variation:

Experiment with other materials and colors when binding the heart. For example, try using a pale pink satin ribbon to add some pretty detail to the finished piece.

deck the halls

When it comes to decorating your home at Christmas, think big, think theatrical, and don't worry about being ever so slightly kitsch. Christmas is about fun, Christmas is about glitz, and it's OK to go just a little over the top. The key to creating impact is to look for materials that are in plentiful supply and easy to get hold of. If you live in the country, that may mean lots of twigs, ivy, and berries; if you're a towns person, you may want to think a little more laterally and make use of fabric scraps, for example, to make some festive bunting.

Christmas bunting

Make a visual splash with some festive bunting that is a refreshing change from traditional paper chains. This project needn't be expensive either as you can easily make it up using the scraps of fabric in your sewing box. Cotton dress fabrics work well, and, even if the motifs aren't seasonal, by choosing typical Christmas colors, such as red and green, you can quickly create a festive ambience. Or, if your Christmas style is rather more glitzy, make up some organza bunting in rich silver, bronze, or gold. Hanging ceiling lights or chandeliers make useful central points to fix the bunting to, but make sure the fabric falls well clear of any light bulbs to avoid the risk of fire.

Materials

To make up about 15yd (14m) bunting with 90 flags

- Template materials (see p. 120)
- ¹/₂yd (50cm) dress cotton in each of three designs
- Pinking shears
- Eyelet pliers
- 200 gold or silver eyelets to fit pliers
- 16yd (15m) ric rac

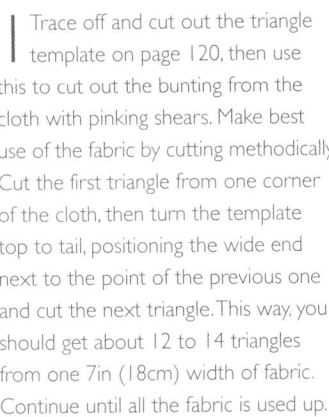

1 Trace off and cut out the triangle template on page 120, then use this to cut out the bunting from the cloth with pinking shears. Make best use of the fabric by cutting methodically. Cut the first triangle from one corner of the cloth, then turn the template top to tail, positioning the wide end next to the point of the previous one and cut the next triangle. This way, you should get about 12 to 14 triangles from one 7in (18cm) width of fabric. Continue until all the fabric is used up.

2 Take two triangles cut from the same fabric and place them wrong sides together with the shortest side of the triangle at the top. Using the eyelet pliers, follow the manufacturer's instructions to place an eyelet ³/₄in (2cm) down from the top edge and ³/₄in (2cm) in from each side.

3 Cut the ric rac to a length that will suit your room, allowing some extra for fixing the bunting in place. Carefully thread the ric rac through each eyelet on the bunting triangles. Tie up in position.

stair garland

Decorating the banisters with a garland brings a festive welcome to the hallway. If you don't want to complicate matters with florist's foam and keeping the foliage damp, you have to either limit yourself to a very short-lived garland, or choose materials that don't depend on much water to stay looking fresh. This garland is made mainly of twigs with the addition of ivy trails and pine, both of which will stay looking fresh for more than a week, given a daily spritz of water. Dried apples and red gingham ribbon add color, whilst a lighting chain adds a bit of sparkle.

Start by making up bundles of three dried apple slices. Pass a quarter of the stub wire through the apples all near the rind, then twist the short end around the longer end to secure in position.

Materials

- 1 pack dried apple slices
- Florist's stub wires or fine-gauge garden wire
- Natural twigs
- White-sprayed twigs
- Pruning shears
- Pine branches
- Trailing ivy
- Wire-edge red gingham ribbon, 1½in (3.5cm) wide, cut into 12in (30cm) lengths
- Raffia
- Lighting chain to fit the length of the banisters

*variation:

You can create completely different looks using the same twiggy and trailing ivy base, by varying the finishing touches. Instead of the apples and gingham ribbon, use dried oranges and cinnamon-stick bundles for a more traditional look, or go for gold by spraying up some cones and teaming with gold wire-edge ribbon.

2 Make up bundles of twigs—natural and white—to fit the length of the banisters and wire them together using more stub wires. Neaten the bundles with pruning shears if necessary.

3 Add in lengths of pine and trailing ivy, then fix into position with more stub wires.

4 Wire the apples into position along the length of the garland, tying on a piece of ribbon next to each apple bundle. Tie the garland to the banisters using the raffia, then add in more greenery to fill out the garland and hide the fixings. Finally, add in the lighting chain down the length of the banisters.

mantel arrangement

Create a frosty winter wonderland around silvered glass candlesticks using classic greenery, white-sprayed twigs, and silvery contorted willow. The silvery decorations tied on with the narrowest of gingham ribbon add interest whilst teaming with the silver candlesticks. It's an arrangement that will last well through the whole Christmas break and, with its natural forest feel, looks great in the hallway, lending the sense of bringing some of the outside in.

Materials

- 5 blocks of florist's foam
- 4 florist's foam trays or plastic boxes
- Florist's tape
- 2 branches of lichen twigs
- Pruning shears
- Large bundle of natural twigs
- Large bundle of white-sprayed twigs
- Branches of pine
- Trailing ivy
- 6 stems of silver sequin-covered contorted willow
- 3 silver candlesticks
- 3 white candles
- Silver heart decorations
- Narrow gingham ribbon cut to 6in (15cm) lengths

1 Soak the florist's foam blocks for a minimum of one hour to ensure they are completely wet through. Next, set them up on the mantel in plastic trays. In the middle of the mantel, place two blocks side by side with one centered on top, then put a block on either side of the stack. Tape them in position using the florist's tape.

2 Cut the lichen branches into pieces about 12in (30cm) long using the pruning shears and push the ends into the foam blocks near the lower edges. In the same way, fix the natural twigs between the lichen twigs.

Inexpensive metal hearts bring delightful decoration to the arrangement. Tied on using a narrow ribbon in tiny purple check, they add charm, whilst linking into the gingham theme of the stair garland.

3 Next, cut the white-sprayed twigs to about 12in (30cm) in length and add a new layer above the natural and lichen twigs.

4 Now cut the pine branches into pieces about 8in (20cm) long and fix them between the twigs, covering up the florist's foam.

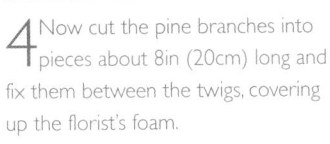

5 Next, add the long lengths of trailing ivy, fixing them between the pieces of pine and the twigs to give body to the arrangement.

6 Add in the silver, sequin-covered contorted willow to give the arrangement a frosted feel.

7 Place the silver candlesticks on top of the foam blocks. Cut some smaller pieces of pine to a length of about 6in (15cm) and use it to cover up the top of the blocks.

8 Finally, tie on pretty silver hearts using short lengths of narrow gingham ribbon.

cross-stitch cushion

Make up a Christmas cross-stitch sampler to give as a special gift, or to keep and bring out every year for the festive season. You can choose a typically Christmas icon, or use a traditional motif, such as this eighteenth-century reindeer, which wouldn't look out of place well into spring. Reindeer worked in a soft red against white have a traditional Scandinavian feel, which works well both in traditional and modern interiors, and especially with the shabby-chic style. Here, the cushion cover was made up using an antique linen napkin that had striped borders in a similar shade to the worked reindeer. If you don't want to go to the trouble of making a cushion cover from scratch, you can mount the worked cross-stitch onto a store-bought cover, using ribbon or braid to stitch it into position.

Materials

- 28ct/in (11ct/cm) evenweave embroidery fabric at least 12 × 8in (30 × 20cm) or 14ct/in (6ct/cm) Aida embroidery fabric at least 20 × 12in (50 × 30cm)
- 2 skeins stranded cotton embroidery floss for the evenweave or 4 skeins if you are using Aida
- Embroidery needle
- Scissors

Working the reindeer

These reindeer have been worked in the traditional way using two threads of stranded embroidery floss on evenweave fabric, which has a perfectly even weft. The crosses are worked over two vertical and two horizontal threads to make a perfectly square cross, with the upper threads all lying in the same direction for an even finish. The design is worked by following the chart, counting two threads for each cross.

Working cross-stitch

Start by working a line of running stitches down the center of the linen in both directions to correspond with the centers marked on the chart. These threads will be removed when the embroidery is complete, so it may be easier to use a contrast color. Work one reindeer at a time, starting with a front hoof, counting out from the center. Once you have started, build up the design in rows.

Evenweave is a fine fabric that beginners may initially find difficult to work with. Aida is another popular fabric suitable for cross-stitch, and first-timers may prefer to use this because it has a larger, basketwork-style weave that makes counting the threads much easier. It is available in 14 to 18ct/in (6 to 7ct/cm). Since the design is worked over counted threads, the size of each cross will depend on the density of the weave, and this will, in turn affect the overall finished size. Worked on 28ct/in (11ct/cm) evenweave, as here, the design works out to be 8 × 4in (20 × 10cm). On 14ct/in (6ct/cm) Aida, the finished piece would be double the size.

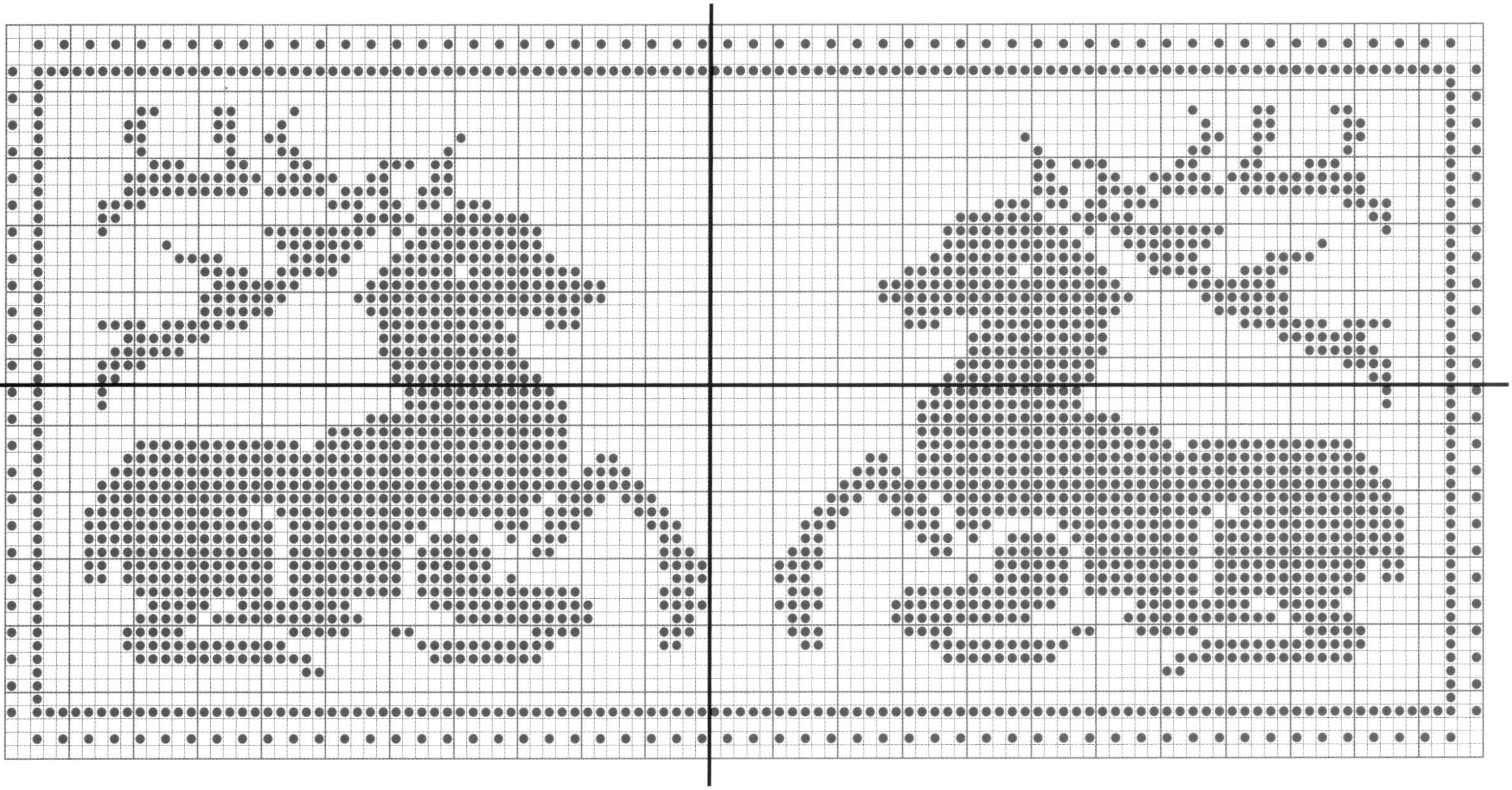

advent calendar

A decorative garland, made up of delicate translucent envelopes clipped onto gold cord, is a delightful alternative to the traditional advent calendar. You don't have to number all the envelopes—every fourth one is enough—and that leaves room for some to be adorned with simple Christmas symbols made from recycled paper. Fill each one with a little gift, or with a heartfelt quotation, motto, or message for your loved ones.

Materials

- Template materials (see p. 120)
- 1 sheet each recycled colored papers in blue, green, pink, brown
- Pencil and gold pen
- Scissors
- 2 × large sheets (A2 size, or approx 16½ × 24in/ 42 × 60cm) heavy-gauge tracing paper or other translucent paper
- Steel ruler
- Scalpel or craft knife
- Glue stick
- Gold pen
- 24 small gifts or mottos
- 6½yd (6m) gold twine
- 26 curtain clips, preferably with small hooks

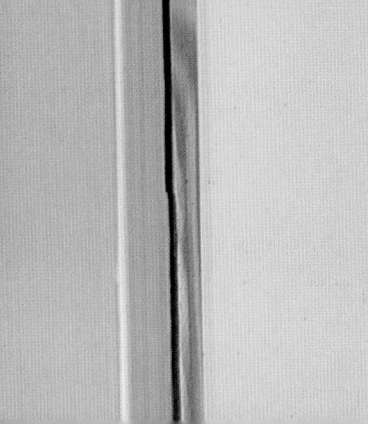

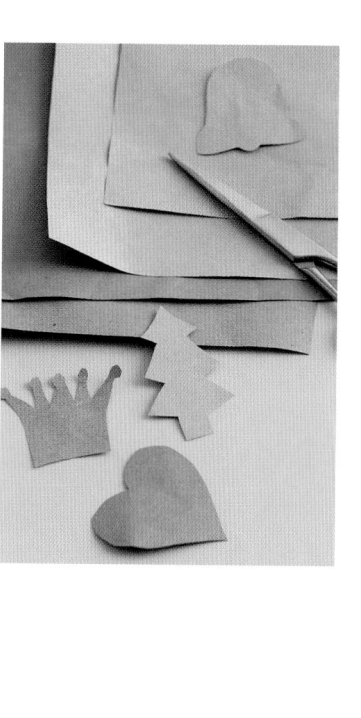

1 Trace off the heart, crown, star, tree, and bell templates on page 121, and use them to cut out the five shapes using a piece of recycled paper. Repeat the process with the other three sheets of colored paper, cutting only four shapes each time to give 17 in total.

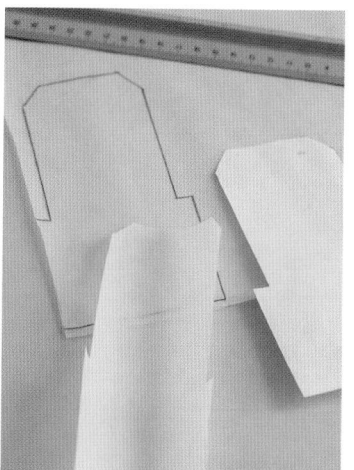

2 Trace off the package template from page 121 and use this to cut 26 templates from translucent paper with either some scissors or a steel rule and scalpel.

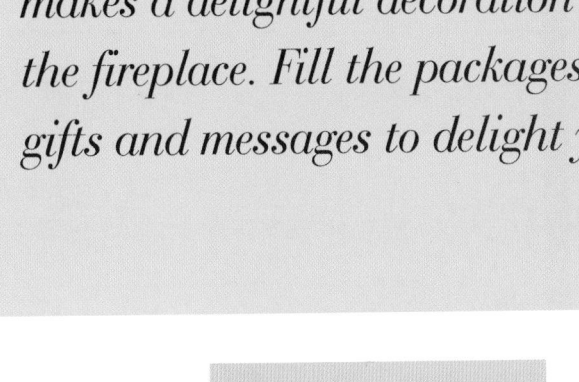

This pretty "grown-up" advent calendar makes a delightful decoration strung above the fireplace. Fill the packages with thoughtful gifts and messages to delight you family.

3 Using a scalpel, gently score along the folds of each package shape as indicated on the template by dotted lines. Fold along the score lines. Run a line of glue along the tabs, fold down the long end, and press firmly to fix.

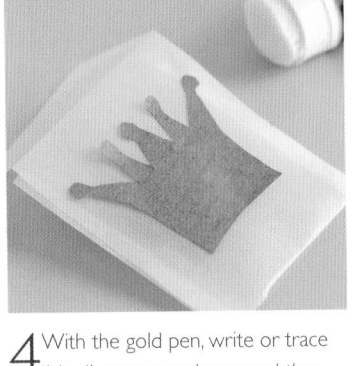

4 With the gold pen, write or trace 'Noel' on two packages and the numbers 1, 4, 8, 12, 20, and 24 on six of the others. Glue the recycled paper templates to the remainder of the packages. Place a motto or gift into each package.

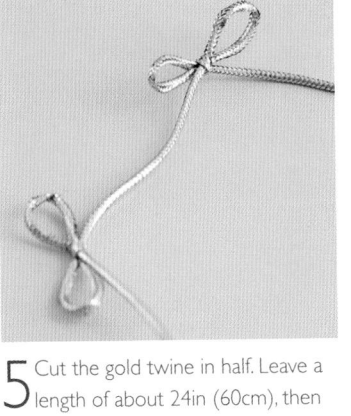

5 Cut the gold twine in half. Leave a length of about 24in (60cm), then tie a small bow in the twine. Now, tie 13 small bows at 4in (10cm) intervals. Repeat with the other piece of twine.

6 Hook a curtain clip into the knot of each bow. Next, clip on the packages, starting with the Noel package, followed by the number 1, two motifs, number 4, three motifs, number 8, three motifs, and so on, finishing with the second Noel package for Christmas Day. Tie the two pieces of twine together in a loop toward the ends, allowing extra length for one piece so that one chain will hang lower. Hang in position, trimming the ends of the twine if necessary.

Christmas-card chandelier

Receiving cards from friends and family near and far offers treasured moments in the frantic run up to Christmas. But cards pose a problem—where to put them once the surfaces are full? This chandelier offers a delightful solution. Highly decorative in itself, it can be left in place after Christmas to become a feature of the room, whilst for the duration of the season, cards hung high can't be knocked or blown over. The chandelier can be made to accommodate as many clips as you like. Make one, two, three, or even more for high-level decorative interest.

Materials

- Reel of 1mm galvanized wire
- Round-nose pliers
- Reel of 28–gauge (0.4mm) beading wire
- 18 × ¼in (6mm) round glass beads
- 9 × 1in (25mm) glass beads
- 18 × ½in (12mm) flat glass beads
- 9 round glass seed beads
- 9 × 1¼in (30mm) alligator clips
- 1½yd (1.5m) wire-edged silver ribbon

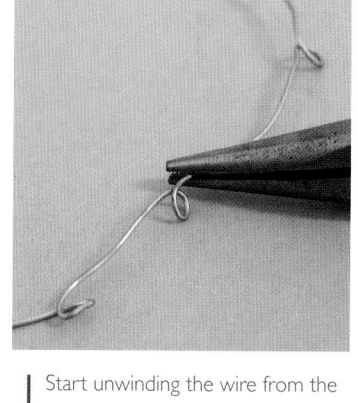

1 Start unwinding the wire from the reel and make eyelets by forming loops along the length with the pliers. Make the first eyelet 6in (15cm) from the end of the wire, then make more loops at 3in (7.5cm) intervals until you have nine loops. Allow another 6in (15cm) at the end and cut off the wire from the reel.

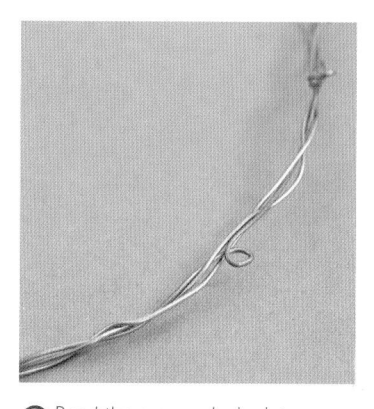

2 Bend the prepared wire into a circle so the first and last eyelets are 3in (7.5cm) apart, then wind the excess wire together to fix in place. Cut another piece of wire about 1½yd (1.5m) long and wind this around the original circle.

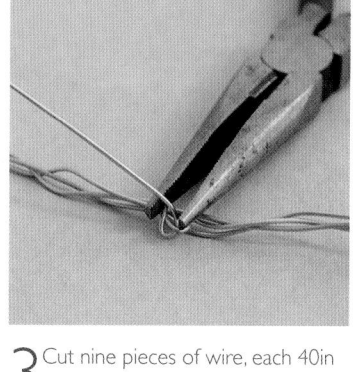

3 Cut nine pieces of wire, each 40in (1m) long and another nine pieces, each 20in (50cm) long. Feed the end of one short wire through an eyelet on the main circle. Using the round-nose pliers, make a loop to fix this end into position and lay it toward the center of the circle. Repeat with the other short wires, fixing them to every other eyelet.

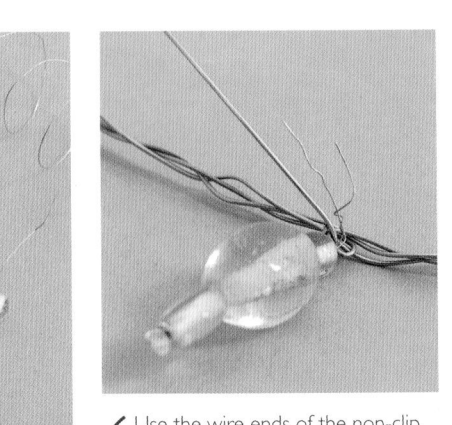

Wire-edged silver ribbon teams well with the galvanized wire and makes a flirty finish for the bottom of the chandelier.

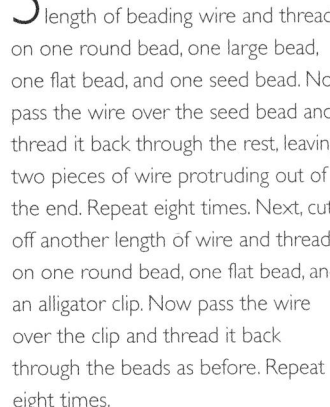

4 At one end of each of the longer pieces of wire use the pliers to make a spiral. Feed the straight ends of these wires into the spare eyelets, then bend the non-spiral ends back in a gentle semicircle to the center of the main circle. At the center, bend the remaining length straight upwards to create the central core.

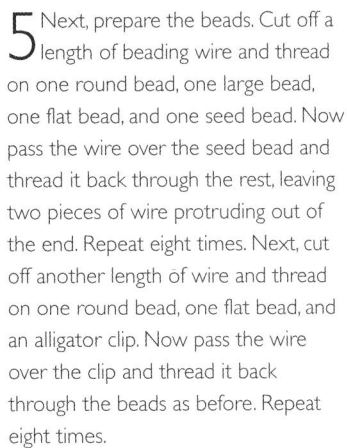

5 Next, prepare the beads. Cut off a length of beading wire and thread on one round bead, one large bead, one flat bead, and one seed bead. Now pass the wire over the seed bead and thread it back through the rest, leaving two pieces of wire protruding out of the end. Repeat eight times. Next, cut off another length of wire and thread on one round bead, one flat bead, and an alligator clip. Now pass the wire over the clip and thread it back through the beads as before. Repeat eight times.

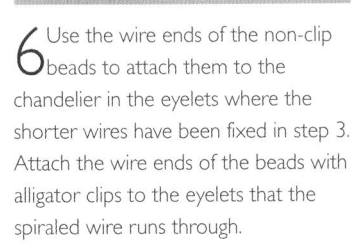

6 Use the wire ends of the non-clip beads to attach them to the chandelier in the eyelets where the shorter wires have been fixed in step 3. Attach the wire ends of the beads with alligator clips to the eyelets that the spiraled wire runs through.

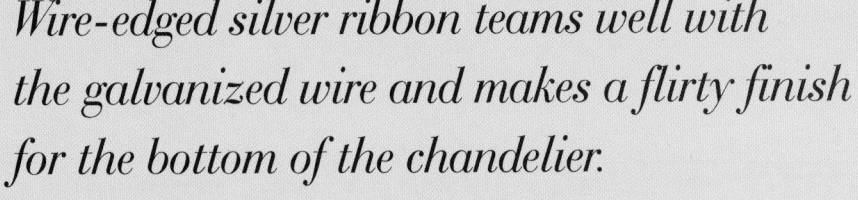

7 Stand the chandelier on a flat surface, gather up all the wire struts, and fix them together near the top using a short piece of galvanized wire. The bends in the spiraled wires should be gathered together at the center of the chandelier. Fix these in place using a 12in (30cm) piece of the wire-edged silver ribbon and leave the ends free.

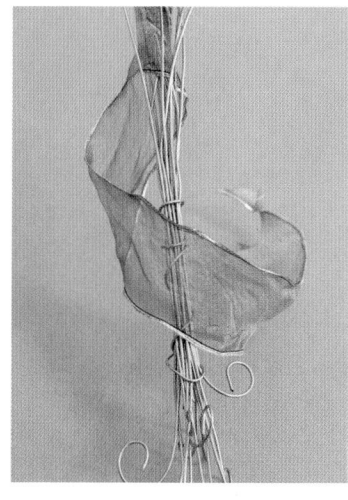

8 Use the remainder of the silver ribbon to bind the stalk of the chandelier and tie at the bottom with a knot, leaving the ends free.

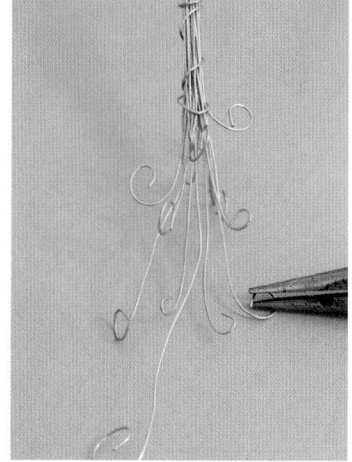

9 At the top of the chandelier, cut the wires to random lengths, then use the pliers to make a curl at the end of each one.

Kissing Doves

This kissing dove garland makes
an elegant decoration for the
mantelpiece or any other focal
point of the room. With its clean,
unfussy lines and soft, muted shades,
it is reminiscent of Shaker style,
which works well in both modern
and traditional homes. Doves have
been symbolic of peace and love
to many religions for thousands of
years. They have also become a
popular Christmas icon, representing
peace on Earth. Olive branches, also
symbolic of peace, are used to
suspend the doves, but if you can't
find these, any twiggy branches
would do.

kissing doves decoration

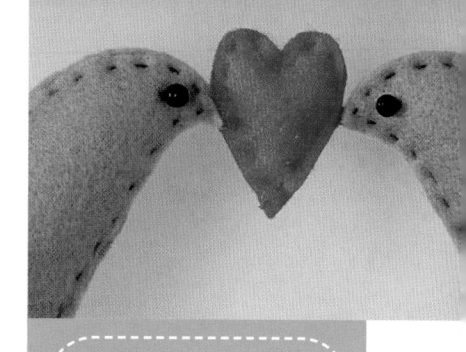

The elegant lines and simple construction of this dove garland mean you're guaranteed a professional result, even if you have only the most basic of sewing skills. If you can sew on a button, you'll be able to make this timeless decoration! The doves' muted tones are typical of the Shaker palette, yet the red heart and ribbon trimming transform the softened blues and grays into an altogether Christmassy feel. The olive twigs add a fresh feel whilst also alluding to the olive twig, which symbolizes reconciliation, often associated with dove imagery.

Materials

- Template materials (see p. 120)
- Fabric scissors
- 2 pieces of gray felt at least 10 × 10in (25 × 25cm)
- 1 piece of blue felt at least 10 × 3in (25 × 8cm)
- Scraps of red felt
- 4 small black beads
- 4 shell buttons
- Sewing needle and black thread
- Stranded embroidery floss in aquamarine and red
- Toy fiberfill
- 2 large olive twigs or similar, such as eucalyptus
- 1yd (1m) red tape or ribbon

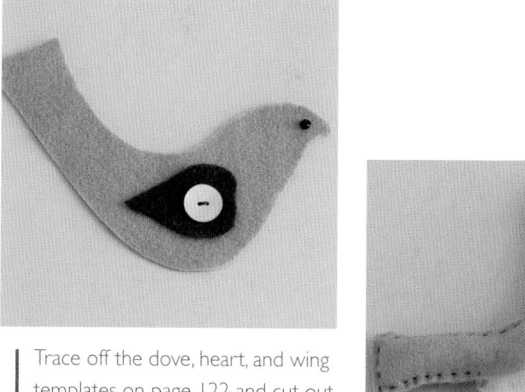

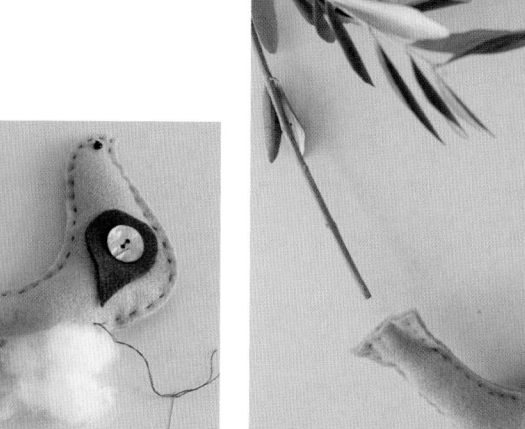

1 Trace off the dove, heart, and wing templates on page 122 and cut out a paper pattern for each. Cut out four dove shapes in gray felt, four wings in blue felt, and two heart shapes in red felt. Lay out the dove shapes so that two face in one direction and two in the other. Sew a black bead in the eye position and sew one button on top of a wing shape in the wing position of each felt dove shape.

2 Using two strands of embroidery floss, stab stitch all around each dove, leaving a large opening at the center of the bottom seam. Fill the tail with toy fiberfill, and then the body of the dove, working it well into the beak area. Stab stitch to close the opening. In the same way, using red floss, sew the two heart pieces together, fill with toy fiberfill, and stitch up. Complete the center of the garland by stitching a bird to either side of the heart by the beak.

3 Strip the leaves off the first few inches of each olive twig, then work the end into the tail of each dove, behind the stuffing.

4 Cut the red tape in half, tie a bow at the end of each tail where it joins the olive twig, and fix it to the mantelpiece with tape.

Victorian Christmas stocking

Children don't have to have all the fun at Christmas—grown-ups love stockings, too, so whizz up this witty one in the shape of a Victorian boot. The subtly exaggerated proportions and silver bells detail give it an almost cartoon-like quality, so go over the top and make it in rich brocade for a fabulous way to present all those small yet precious gifts. You don't need a lot of fabric, so you can use up trimmings from other home projects, or pick up remnants of otherwise expensive materials to create a sumptuous stocking.

Materials
• Template materials (see p. 120)
• Fabric scissors
• ½yd (50cm) main fabric
• ½yd (50cm) lining fabric
• ½yd (50cm) brocade fabric
• Thread
• Fabric adhesive
• ¾yd (70cm) braid
• Toy fiberfill

1 Trace off the templates on page 123 and cut out two boot shapes in both the main and lining fabrics, plus two shoe shapes and four cuff shapes in the brocade fabric. If the brocade fabric has a border design with an integral selvage, use that for the outside cuff pieces. Stitch a hem along the lower edge of the cuffs (unless you can use the selvage). Baste a cuff piece and shoe piece onto the right side of each main boot piece. Using fabric adhesive, stick the braid over the raw edge at the top shoe edge, then stitch into position. Baste a cuff piece to the right side of each lining piece.

2 With right sides together, place one prepared main piece on top of one lining piece and stitch together at the top edge. Repeat with the other two prepared pieces. Trim the seams and press them open, then clip the curves to allow the seam to lie flat.

3 Open out these prepared pieces and place right sides together so the main pieces match and the lining pieces match. Baste. Stitch the pieces together, starting on the lining near the top of the back seam. Carry on over the top edge seam to the main boot piece. Stitch all around the main piece boot shape, down the front seam of the lining, and across the bottom to the back seam again. Leave a large opening in the lining in the back seam. Trim the seams, press them open, and clip the curves.

4 Turn the main part of the stocking to right sides, then fill the toe and heel with toy fiberfill through the opening in the lining. Slipstitch the lining to close, then push the lining back down into the stocking to finish.

snowman stocking

Children love to bring out their own special stocking every year to hang up on Christmas Eve, so why not help them to make their own individual one? This stocking is a genuine Santa-boot shape—round-toed and generously proportioned; perfect for packing with plenty of presents! The snowman design is always popular with children. This stocking has heart-shaped snowflakes for a girl, but use circular snowflakes to appeal to a boy. If you have more than one child you may also like to incorporate their name in felt letters on the generous contrast cuff.

Materials

- Template materials (see p. 120)
- Fabric scissors
- 2 8 x 12in (20 x 30cm) blue felt rectangles
- ½yd (50cm) red felt
- Fabric adhesive
- Sewing thread in white, black, and blue
- 8 x 12in (20 x 30cm) white felt rectangle
- 2 x ½in (1cm) flat blue sequins
- 6 small black beads
- 3 x red flower-shaped sequins
- 4in (10cm) red spotty ribbon, ¾in (2cm) wide
- 1yd (1m) narrow red ric rac
- ½yd (50cm) narrow gingham ribbon

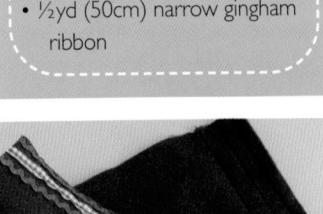

1 Trace off the templates on page 124, then cut out two toe caps and one hat in blue felt., then two boot shapes in red felt. Cut two blue boot cuff pieces measuring 8½ x 6in (22 x 15cm). With the white felt, cut out the shapes for the snowman's head and body, and 25 heart shapes for the snowflakes. Use the adhesive to stick the main body pieces and hat in position on one of the red boot shapes, then use white thread and stab stitch to secure them in place.

2 Next, sew the snowman's features, buttons, and scarf in position, using the blue sequins and two of the black beads for the eyes, one black bead for the nose, the flower-shaped sequins and remaining black beads for the buttons, and the red spotty ribbon for the scarf. Leaving a 5½in (14cm) gap at the top of the boot, stitch the snowflakes into position around the snowman, using one stitch in the center of each heart. Sew ric rac close to the straight edge of the toe cap, then use fabric adhesive to stick these into position on each red boot piece.

3 On one boot cuff piece, stitch a length of ric rac near to the bottom, then a length of gingham ribbon above, followed by another length of ric rac. Repeat with the other cuff piece. Place the right side of one cuff to the wrong side of the top of one boot piece and stitch. Repeat with the other cuff.

4 Place the red main pieces of the boot right sides together. (The cuff pieces should be wrong sides together.) Stitch around the main red pieces of the boot. Turn the boot inside out.

dress the tree

There's something nostalgic about dusting down the decorations at the start of the Christmas season, and perhaps adding a few each year, building up an 'album' of Christmases past. In our family, since the children were tiny, we have traditionally got together with friends at the beginning of December to make the decorations. Yet despite the varied skills of family and friends, we managed to build a tree over the years, dressed with decorations that all looked good together. The secret? We kept to a color scheme. We have added bought lights, and allowed ourselves one bought decoration a year. Many of the decorations on the following pages have been developed over those sessions... so we can guarantee they're quick and easy to make!

treetop decoration

The placing of a special decoration at the top of a beautifully adorned tree marks the arrival of the festive season with style. Try making this easy-to-make yet charming treetop decoration based around the traditional Scandinavian papercrafts also used on page 60. Cut a few strips of paper to make your star, then mount it onto a glossy red background and decorate with tree lights. Simple, yes, but striking!

Materials

- 1 sheet US Letter or A4 paper
- Cutting mat
- Steel ruler
- Scalpel
- Glue stick
- Template materials (see p. 120)
- 1 sheet card at least 12 x 12in (30 x 30cm)
- 1 sheet glossy red gift wrap
- 30in (75cm) chiffon ribbon, 1¼in (3cm) wide
- Hole punch
- Ribbon

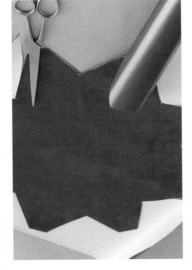

1 Make the star as for the Paper Stars decoration on page 60, but cut the strips ½in (1cm) wide and do not add the ribbon at this stage. Trace off the star pattern on page 125 and cut it out in card. Glue this card shape to the back of the glossy gift wrap, then cut out the shape using the scissors.

2 Now stick this card glossy side up onto the back of the gift wrap again, then cut out another star shape and glue it to the card.

3 Stick the paper star onto one side of the red star shape using the glue stick.

4 Use a hole punch to make a hole in one point of the star. Fold the ribbon in half and pass it through the hole from the back. Loop through. Use this to tie the star to the tree top. Twine lights around the star to finish.

white paper star

Dress a tree for next to nothing with these delicate decorations made from simple white paper . In Finland, children cut up strips of paper to create pretty stars like these. The decorations may initially look complicated, but once you understand how they're put together, you can give the stars different personalities, depending on the paper you use and the length and width of the paper strips. Get the whole family together and, within the afternoon, you'll have enough stars to fill a tree!

Materials

- 1 sheet of US Letter or A4 paper
- Cutting mat
- Pencil
- Steel ruler
- Scalpel
- Glue stick
- Ribbon

1 Position the paper in portrait format on the cutting mat and mark ¼in (5mm) wide strips running down the length of the sheet. Cut the strips using the steel rule and scalpel.

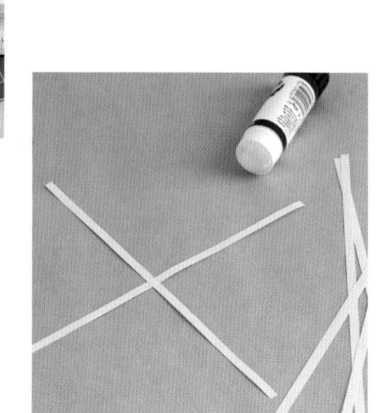

2 Bend two strips in half to find the center and glue them together at this point.

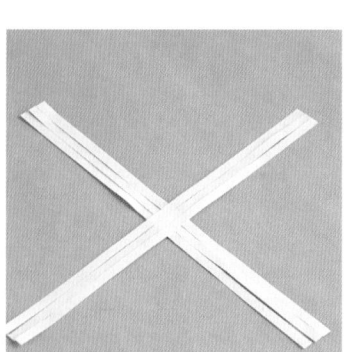

3 Glue one strip of paper on either side of the original strip and repeat with the other original piece to make a cross that is three strips wide.

4 Take two adjacent strips that are on the outside of the points and glue their ends together to form a 'petal'. Repeat with the other three sets of adjacent strips, leaving the central pieces straight. Repeat steps 2 to 4 to make another shape the same.

5 You will now have two similar shapes. Place one on top of the other, so they seem to 'hug' each other, rather than curve away from each other. Position the 'petal' tips of one shape above the straight struts of the other. Glue the two star shapes together in the middle. Now glue the tip of the 'petal' ½in (1cm) from the end of the straight strut to form a point of the star. Repeat with the other points. Cut a length of ribbon 8in (20cm) long and tie it through one point of the star for hanging.

 variation:

You might like to team your paper stars with a few pretty hearts (see left), a favorite Christmas motif in Denmark, which are simply cut from thin white card. You'll find the template for these delightful hearts on page 125. By cutting another smaller heart-shape out of the middle, you will create a lighter, more delicate feel which will also allow the light to shine through. The outlines can be cut with scissors, but it's more effective to cut the central hearts out using a scalpel. Pierce a small hole at the top to thread a hanging ribbon through.

glass bead star

Put up some sparkly stars for a fabulous Christmasy feel. This is the perfect project for little hands to help out with as the star is so simple to make. The star can be made to any size you like—this one measures 7in (18cm) across—and, by using beads of varying sizes and shapes, you can achieve a range of different effects. Pretty and light reflective, glass beads are imported from India and can be bought inexpensively in a wide variety of colors and sizes. (If you can't source a local bead supplier, check on the internet.) For some variation, try bending the wire into various shapes, such as hearts, trees, even simple angel shapes.

Materials

- 42in (105cm) silver-plated 18-gauge jewelry or hobby wire
- Wire cutters
- Pliers
- 54 glass beads about ¹/₂in (1cm) long
- 6 blue glass leaf beads
- Fuse wire
- Scissors
- 28in (70cm) gold twine
- 10in (25cm) organza ribbon, ¹/₂in (12mm) wide

1 Cut the jewelry wire in half, bend one end into a small hook shape with pliers, and thread on 9 of the glass beads. Next, thread on one of the blue leaf beads, then repeat the process twice more. Make a hook at the opposite end of the wire and attach the two ends together. Bend into a triangle with 9 beads on each side. Repeat with the second piece of wire and the rest of the beads.

2 Place one triangle over the other to make a star shape. Use fuse wire to fix the triangles together at the points where they cross. The joints should all be three beads in from every point.

3 Cut the gold twine into six lengths, and tie one length over the wire at every joint to add decoration to the star.

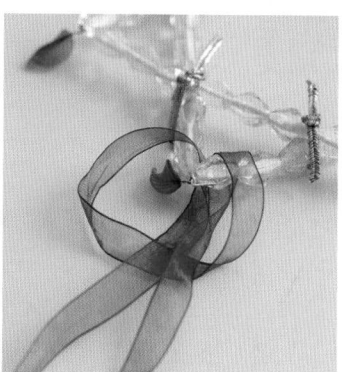

4 Make a ribbon tie by folding the organza in half, passing the folded end through one point of the star, then passing the loose ends through the fold. Pull tight to secure in place.

Tin Can Treats

Transform tin cans into witty decorations. Aluminum drinks cans are surprisingly easy to cut using strong scissors, such as florist's scissors, giving you a wonderful choice of shiny metallic materials all for free. It's a favorite art material in Mexico, but can just as well be used to give a fresh take on traditional Christmas decorations. The little lanterns are a European childhood favorite, usually made from paper, whilst Danish children have traditionally woven little paper heart baskets. Cut from metal, both take on a much more contemporary feel. Get the children to save all their drinks cans and you'll soon get a whole tree-full of decorations for free. Although the metal is not difficult to handle, potentially sharp edges make the material not suitable for young children to use.

green lanterns

These traditional lanterns, based on the paper versions children make in primary school, couldn't be easier. Find some bright shiny green cans for a lively Christmasy color and make some—or even all—inside out for a silvery version. These are an excellent starting point for your first tin can decorations whilst you get used to handling the material.

Materials

To make 2 lanterns and 1 chain
- Tin cans (allow one can for two lanterns and one for the chain)
- Floral scissors or other heavy-duty scissors
- Small stapler
- Sticky tape (optional)

1 Start by cutting off the top of the first can. Put the scissors in through the hole made by the ring pull, then cut around the top just below where the can begins to curve in. Cut down the side of the can, and then cut off the bottom, just above the curve. Fold the resulting rectangle in half lengthwise, then cut this in half along its width.

2 Cut a 'fringe' into the folded side of each length of metal, with each 'fringe' finishing ¹/₂in (1cm) in from the edge.

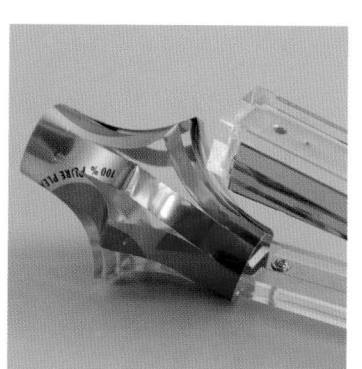

3 Unfold each length of metal and bring the sides together, and you'll see the lanterns begin to take shape. Staple the ends together at the top and the bottom to fix each lantern in position.

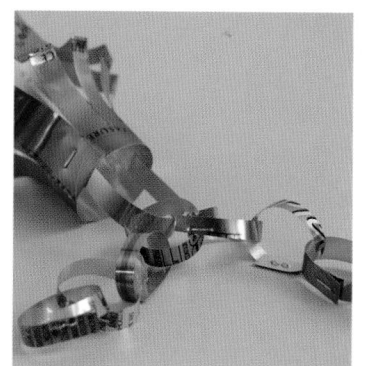

4 Cut another tin can into narrow strips and make a chain, stapling the links together. Use one strip to make a 'handle' by stapling each end to the inside rim of the lantern, and link one of the chain links into this. If you can't manoeuvre the stapler into position, the lantern handle can be fixed with sticky tape.

heart basket

These traditional Danish woven baskets look delightful made from paper, but take on a contemporary recycled feel when made from tin cans. Red is the obvious color, but alternative colors are just as effective. You can emphasize the basket weave by using one piece turned inside out to set off silver against red. Although these are made to the same principles of simple weaving, instead of passing above and below each other, the loops are passed alternately through one loop and around the next. When the heart is finished, you should be able to open it up into a little basket. Do take care not to cut your fingers on any sharp edges.

Materials

- Templates material (see p. 120)
- 2 drinks cans
- Floral scissors or other heavy-duty scissors
- Sticky tape

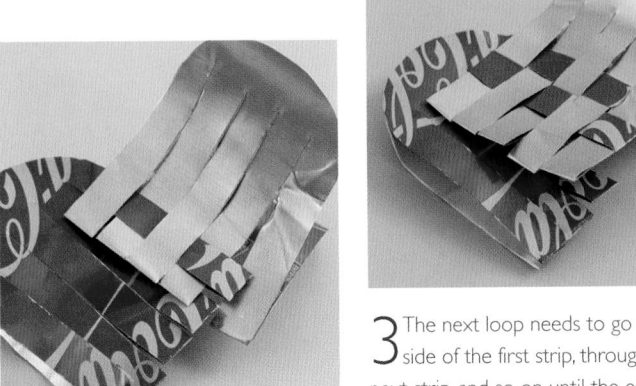

1 Trace off the template on page 125 and cut out in paper. Cut the top and bottom off the can as described in step 1 on page 67, then fold the body of the can in half widthwise rather than lengthwise. Place the template onto the can with the straight edge on the fold and cut it out. Make three long cuts to follow the slits on the template. These cuts must be exact in both their position and length. Repeat with another can so you have two pieces. Fold one inside out if preferred. Use the wastage to cut a handle.

2 Take an end strip from one shape and pass this loop through the first loop of the other shape, then let the loop go either side of the next strip and through the loop of the next. Repeat until you get to the edge of the heart.

3 The next loop needs to go either side of the first strip, through the next strip, and so on until the end. As you work, you'll need to slide the woven loops up as far as you can to provide space to work on the last strips, which can get a little tight.

4 As you work, you will see the heart shape forming. The last pieces to be woven can get a little fiddly, but the tin is robust and can be bent to get it into position. Once the heart is finished, you should be able to open up the basket. If you can't, it will be because some of the strips have been woven over and under instead of through and around the loops. When the basket is finished, fix the handle in place using sticky tape.

Beaded Decorations

Exquisite beaded and sequinned decorations bring a sumptuous, festive feel wherever they're hung—be it on the tree or anywhere else around the house. Being handmade, each one is unique, and to buy them would be prohibitively expensive. Yet they're so easy to make, everyone can join in.

In our family, we've been sequining Christmas balls since the children were very young. It was the ideal combination: the children became surprisingly absorbed and, given a tray of sequins, pins, and a ball, would spend hours creating. Once finished, their wonderful decorations went straight onto the tree, and have been brought out every year for twelve years.

We gave the children the biggest possible sequins for easy handling, but nowadays, in our house, beading decorations has become a rather more sophisticated affair. Friends arrive with old beads and sequins (it's amazing what granny's old costume jewelry can produce!), which we pool with a selection of beads and crafting pins (which are shorter than dressmaking pins), and polystyrene balls, eggs, and hearts, then we all get beading. This year, our beading party ranged from 16 to 74 year olds, and these are some of the results.

sequin ball

This project looks amazing hanging on a tree or from a chandelier, yet it is very quick and easy to make. The combination of gleaming metallics, iridescent turquoise, and azure beads arranged in concentric circles with pointed metal beads top and bottom are reminiscent of the exotic domes of ancient Byzantium.

Materials

- 1 tube each of bronze and gold ¹/₈in (3mm) pearl beads
- 1 tube each of silver, pink, gold, and blue ¹/₄in (5mm) cup sequins
- 1 pack crafting pins or dressmaking pins
- 2in (5cm) polystyrene crafting ball
- 2 small pointed metal beads
- 1 tube of blue round glass beads
- 1 tube of turquoise flat beads
- Chiffon ribbon to hang

1 Thread one bronze pearl bead, then one gold sequin onto a pin and push it into the center of the polystyrene ball, and continue like this until you have made a circle around the circumference. In the same way, make a circle next to that using gold pearl beads and gold sequins, then another gold circle on the other side of the bronze beads. You should now have a center band of three rows of sequins and beads: a middle bronze one, with a gold row on either side

2 Put a pointed metal bead onto a pin and fix into the South Pole position. Next make two circles of blue sequins. Finish the underside by covering it with silver sequins.

3 Turn the ball over, and start by placing a pointed metal bead in the North Pole position. Next fix in one row of silver sequins, two rows of pink sequins, two rows of blue round glass beads, and finally three rows of flat turquoise beads. Note that sequins cover the polystyrene very well and can easily be slightly overlapped. Sometimes, the polystyrene glares through from between round beads, so slip a sequin under these, as shown in step 1. If small flat beads like the turquoise beads don't cover well, simply add some on top of others to cover the polystyrene.

4 Remove the metal bead at the North Pole position, thread a length of ribbon onto the pin for hanging, and a sequin to act as a washer, then replace the pin in the polystyrene ball.

*variation:

Sequin balls are so easy to make, even children can do it, but under-tens should be supervised at all times, and it's not recommended for under-fives, who may put pins in their mouths. Choose the biggest sequins you can find—$^{1}/_{2}$in (1cm) in diameter—in a range of colors that all look good together. That way, the children are guaranteed a fabulous finished decoration. They usually start by putting in the sequins randomly, though older age groups soon graduate to doing concentric circles as shown above.

knitted tree pets

Create some cute knitted characters to bring personality to your tree. If you've mastered the art of plain knitting and you can cast on and cast off, you'll have these Christmas creatures made in a trice. Both the reindeer and the poodle are made from the same basic pattern, and a ribbon collar added for a cute finish. You can knit several of each to fill the tree, or develop your own characters. The key is to choose animals with distinguishing features—such as a dachshund, which you could make by following the poodle pattern and elongating the body and tail, whilst shortening the legs. A giraffe would have elongated legs and neck plus little horns and ears. Exaggerate their distinguishing features to give them an appealing cartoon-like quality

Rudolph Reindeer

Felt antlers and ears give Rudolph his undeniable reindeer character. Best of all, they simply need to be cut out and stitched into position!

BODY
Cast on 30 stitches, knit 22 rows, cast off.
HEAD
Cast on 10 stitches, knit 26 rows, cast off.
MUZZLE
Fold head piece in half to find center. Pick up and knit 9 stitches from one edge of the center section. Knit 1 row. Knit two together at the beginning of the next 6 rows. Cast off.
LEGS
Cast on 10 stitches, knit 14 rows, cast off.
Knit three more legs in the same way
TO MAKE UP
Fold the body section in half and, using a darning needle and the knitting yarn, oversew the front and the underside. Fill with toy fiberfill and oversew to close.
Roll up a leg and oversew down the long seam. Repeat with other three legs. Stitch the legs to the body.
Oversew the back seam of the head. Oversew

the front seam from the neck edge upwards and under the chin to the end of the nose. Fill with toy fiberfill from the back and oversew to close.
Stitch the head to the body pointing forward at an angle.
Make a small tassel from knitting yarn for the tail and stitch in position.
Trace off the antler and ear templates on page 126 and cut two ears and four antler pieces in red felt. Place one antler piece on top of another and, using two strands of red embroidery floss, make a line of running stitches down the center to stitch them together. Repeat for the other antler. Stitch into position at the top of the head. Fold an ear piece in half lengthwise and stitch to the side of one antler. Repeat with the other ear. Stitch the large bead at the end of the nose. Stitch the two small beads onto the face for eyes. Tie on the ribbon collar, thread through some yarn, tie, and use this to hang the decoration.

Materials

- Templates materials (see p. 120)
- Fabric scissors
- 1 ball red cotton DK
- 1 pair knitting needles USA size 3 (UK10/3.35)
- Darning needle
- Toy fiberfill
- Scrap of red felt
- Red embroidery floss
- Embroidery needle
- 1 black bead for nose
- Black sewing thread
- 2 tiny black beads for eyes
- Ribbon for collar

Tie a jolly red collar onto a snowy white poodle and, hey presto, a festive pet to join the traditional Christmas favorites!

Polly Poodle

Fluffy sections, an elongated nose and eyes just-a-touch too close together add up to slightly exaggerated poodle vital statistics, giving Polly a quirky, cartoon-like quality.

BODY

Using cotton DK, cast on 30 stitches, knit 2 rows. Change to fluffy yarn, knit 12 rows. Change to cotton yarn, knit 7 rows. Change to fluffy yarn, knit 12 rows. Cast off.

HEAD

Using cotton DK, cast on 10 stitches, knit 10 rows. Change to fluffy yarn, knit 12 rows. Change to cotton yarn, knit 10 rows. Cast off.

MUZZLE

Fold the head piece in half to find the center. Pick up and knit 9 stitches from one edge of the center section. Knit 2 rows. Knit two together at the beginning of the next 2 rows. Knit 1 row. Knit two together at the beginning of the next 2 rows. Knit 1 row. Knit two together at the beginning of the next 2 rows. Cast off.

LEGS

Using cotton DK, cast on 10 stitches, knit 10 rows. Change to fluffy yarn, knit 4 rows. Change to cotton yarn, knit 14 rows. Cast off.
Knit three more legs in the same way.

TAIL

Using cotton DK, cast on 6 stitches, knit 11 rows. Change to fluffy yarn, knit 11 rows. Change to cotton yarn, knit 7 rows. Cast off.

EARS

Using cotton DK, cast on 10 stitches, knit 10 rows. Cast off. Repeat for the other ear.

TO MAKE UP

Fold the body section in half and, using a darning needle and the knitting yarn, oversew the front and the underside. Fill with toy fiberfill and oversew to close.

Roll up a leg and oversew down the long seam. Repeat with other three legs. Stitch the legs to the body with the fluffy section at the paw end.

Roll up the tail and oversew along the long seam. Stitch in position at an angle.

Oversew the back seam of the head. Oversew the front seam from the neck edge upward and under the chin to the end of the nose. Fill the head with toy fiberfill from the back and oversew to close. Stitch to the body in a vertical position for a poodle-like posture.

Sew the ears onto the head, lining them up just below the fluffy section on the head.

Stitch the large bead at the end of the nose using black thread.

Stitch the two small beads onto the face for eyes.

Tie on the ribbon collar, thread through some yarn, tie, and use this to hang the decoration.

Christmas entertaining

Setting a festive table does not necessarily mean you have to buy special seasonal tableware. It's more a case of using and adapting what you have, then adding a touch of inexpensive sparkle. The following pages show just what is possible using ordinary white china, white linens, and everyday glassware to create lots of quick and easy ideas and three very different overall looks. All the ideas can be mixed, matched, and adapted by using different materials, to provide endless creative possibilities.

jingle bells table

Red and gold make a wonderful Christmas combination, and can be used in a light, contemporary way like this, or given a more traditional feel with the addition of lush pine leaves and cones. Here, everyday glass tableware has been given some Christmas glitz with a gold runner, handmade crackers, gold-cord napkin ties, gold card place names, and a simple wreath of ivy around the votives. Inexpensive reindeer ornaments have been given jingle-bell necklaces made from the runner trim.

Ideas

• Rub a light touch of picture framer's gold fingering onto dainty ivy leaves to make a simple 'wreath' to surround each votive.

• Make festive Christmas tree place names cut from gold card using the template on page 126. Stand them up using gold or red office clips, available from any stationer.

• Use gold cord to tie up starched white linen napkins like elegant Christmas parcels. Knot the ends to prevent unraveling and to provide design interest.

festive cracker

Crackers always provide festive impact. By making your own you can buy the paper to add exactly the colors you want, with delightful, unique decorations and detail. You can also fill them with meaningful gifts (or even pretty candy), so there's more fun in pulling them. Choose a soft paper that will be flexible and easier to manage at the points where the crackers need to be tied. Memory twine is a wonderful material for decorating the crackers as it will stay in any shape that you bend it. It's available in good haberdashers, but if you can't get hold of any, you can use gold wire as a substitute.

Materials

- Paper glue or double-sided tape
- 2 cardboard tubes
- 1 sheet colorful paper 13 × 6in (33 × 15cm)
- Scissors
- Gift
- Cracker snap
- 24in (60cm) wire-edged organza ribbon, 1½in (4cm) wide
- 15in (38cm) memory twine
- Pen

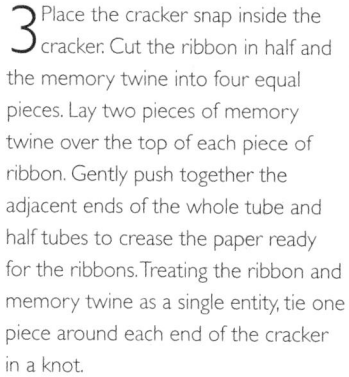

1 Put a line of glue along the length of one cardboard tube and place it horizontally in the middle of the paper close to the long edge nearest to you. Next, cut the second tube in half, then stick the two pieces 1½in (4cm) from each end of the whole roll. Make sure the rough cut ends are facing inward to ensure a neater finish.

2 Put a gift into the whole cardboard tube. Run a line of glue along the far long edge of the paper, then roll it up and press along the glue line to fix.

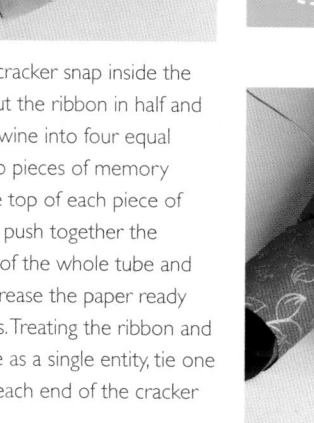

3 Place the cracker snap inside the cracker. Cut the ribbon in half and the memory twine into four equal pieces. Lay two pieces of memory twine over the top of each piece of ribbon. Gently push together the adjacent ends of the whole tube and half tubes to crease the paper ready for the ribbons. Treating the ribbon and memory twine as a single entity, tie one piece around each end of the cracker in a knot.

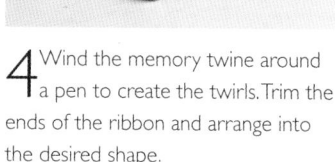

4 Wind the memory twine around a pen to create the twirls. Trim the ends of the ribbon and arrange into the desired shape.

gold table runner

Throw a gold table runner over everyday tablecloths for an instantly festive feel. Making your own runner means you can cut it to size, fitting your table exactly: it won't take long to run up, and is very likely to be less expensive than one bought from a store. This one is made from delicate, light-reflecting translucent organza, lending more of a gold-dust feel to the table, rather than a sense of heavy opulence. The runner is made up of two layers—one in gold, the other in bronze—for a sense of depth. Silver braid adorned with tiny silver bells makes a delightful fun trimming running down the long sides. In contrast, the short ends of the runner have been kept elegantly simple with rows of topstitching.

Materials

- Gold organza to fit the length of your table, plus at least 6in (15cm)—depending on the size of your chosen overhang
- Tape measure
- Bronze organza the same length as the gold
- Fabric scissors
- Gold sewing thread
- Needle
- Braid twice the length of the finished length of the runner plus 1in (2.5cm)

1 First, measure the gold organza to fit the length of your table, adding any overhang you would like at the end of the table. Next, measure the width, making the organza at least 14in (35cm) wide—you can adjust this according to the size of your table—then cut out the fabric. Cut the bronze organza to the same length.

2 Place the lengths of gold and bronze organza right sides together and, using gold thread, stitch all around, leaving an opening at one end. Trim the seams, press them open, and turn the runner through to right sides. Slip stitch the opening on the short side to close. Stitch braid along both long sides.

3 Using gold thread, make three rows of topstitching along each of the long sides of the runner close to the braid edge.

4 On the short sides, make several rows of gold topstitching for an elegant, restrained finish.

Ideas

• Pine cones, lightly sprayed white, add natural seasonal decoration, whilst antique-silvered glass balls lend a little sparkle. So easy, yet so effective!

• Even ice cubes can benefit from the decorative touch. Put a few cranberries in the ice trays before freezing the water to add a warm red color to your ice-cold drinks. And if you don't use them all this year, they'll keep well until next!

• Rose blooms might not immediately be associated with Christmas, but rich red ones can be used to bring a pretty splash of color to a Scandinavian-themed table, toning with the other accessories.

Scandinavian table

Ancient midwinter festivals of light have traditionally held a special significance in Scandinavia, especially in the far north, where the sun doesn't even make it over the horizon. And as Christmas replaced the pagan festivals of old, many of the light festival traditions were adopted to take on Christian significance. Many centuries later, these traditions crossed the Atlantic with Lutheran Protestants from the Scandinavian countries. The style is hallmarked by light-reflective pale- and natural-colored tableware, an abundance of candlelight, and splashes of red. This setting combines natural linens and simple white china with hallmark red detailing and natural pine cones to give a frosty finish. The centerpiece is made of readily available cranberries in a bowl, entwined by delicate trails of variegated ivy. Dressed-up recycled glass jars, scattered all over the table in a celebration of light, make ideal and inexpensive candle votives.

beaded napkin decoration

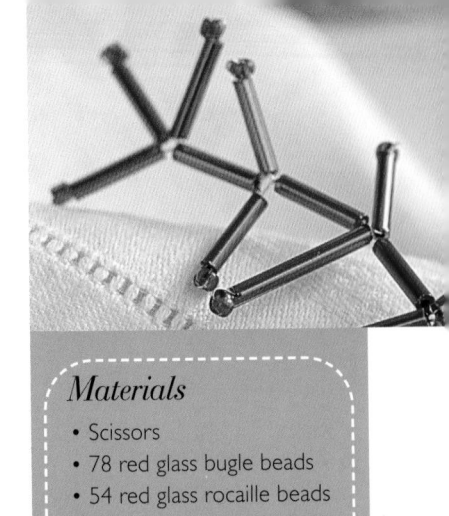

Delicate snowflakes, used here to decorate napkins, make a delightful Christmas motif. Made from red glass beads, they're inexpensive and surprisingly easy to construct, despite their intricate and fragile appearance. Charming in a family four-place setting, they'd look just as attractive set out in serried ranks on either side of a long refectory-style table. Keep the look simple, Scandinavian style, by tying the snowflakes in place using natural string that blends in well with the white napkins.

Materials

- Scissors
- 78 red glass bugle beads
- 54 red glass rocaille beads
- 3yd (3m) fine copper beading wire
- String

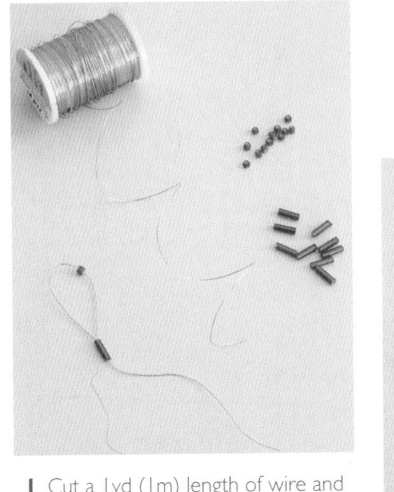

1 Cut a 1yd (1m) length of wire and thread on one rocaille. Push it down to the middle of the wire. Thread both ends of the wire through one bugle bead and push down tight to the rocaille.

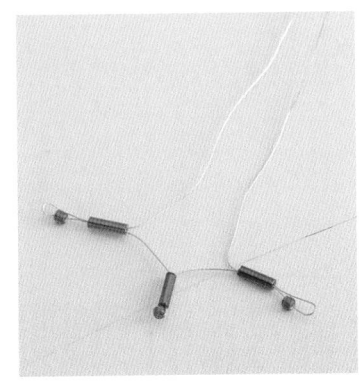

2 Thread one bugle bead and one rocaille onto each end of the beading wire. Pass the wire over the rocaille and back through the bugle. Pull the wires tight.

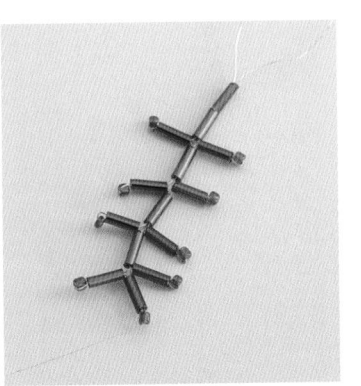

3 Pass both ends of the wire through a bugle bead. Repeat steps 2 and 3 three times. Pass both ends of the wire through another bugle bead.

4 Repeat step 2 and then pass both ends of the wire through a bugle bead. Repeat three times. Pass one wire through a rocaille, then pass the wire over it and back through the last bugle bead. Pass the other wire through any bugle and trim the ends.

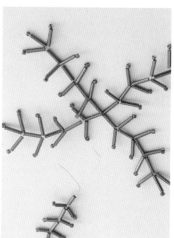

6 In the same way, make a third spoke, joining it to the center of the snowflake. Tie it in position around the napkin using string.

5 In the same way, make another 'spoke' of the snowflake, but when you come to the halfway point, pass one wire over the first 'spoke' between the two central bugle beads, and one underneath it, then continue to finish the 'spoke'.

decorated votive

Candlelight is a key element in Scandinavian design and you really can't use too much, so, instead, go overboard and make a statement with it. The simplest ideas are often the most effective, so collect glass jars and decorate them to use as votives. Small ones like these, originally used for yoghurt, are particularly appealing, but look, too, for mustard, olive, or any other neat glass containers that can be decorated. They don't have to be identical shapes and sizes: if you decorate them all in the same way, they will take on an homogenous look and their differences will only serve to add interest.

Materials

- Scissors
- Rectangular paper doilies
- Small recycled glass jars
- Red giftwrap
- Gluestick
- String
- Tea light

1 Using scissors, cut off the 'lace' edges of the paper doily and cut it to length to fit around the glass jar.

2 In the same way, cut a rectangular piece of red giftwrap to wrap around the jar.

3 Wrap the piece of giftwrap around the jar and stick in position using a glue stick. Repeat with the length of paper doily.

4 Cut a length of string and tie around the jar using a reef knot. Trim the ends for a neat finish. Drop a tea light into the bottom of the jar.

gold table

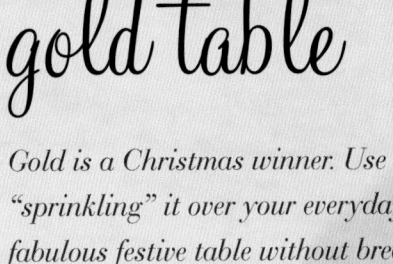

Gold is a Christmas winner. Use it like stardust, "sprinkling" it over your everyday tableware to create a fabulous festive table without breaking the bank. There are many ways to add gold, all of which are readily available in the run-up to Christmas. You can either go for a strong, opulent look, teaming it with traditional greenery, such as holly and fir, or you can keep it lighter, as here, bringing a translucent golden touch to the table, which has a more contemporary feel. Look for gold organza to use as table coverings, gold, silver, or bronze metallic ribbons, plus gorgeous gold card and giftwrap, and you'll have the main ingredients for your stunning golden look.

Ideas

• Slip some skeletonized magnolia leaves under a translucent gold organza cloth. It's an easy way to add interest at table level and goes brilliantly with the King's Crown Plates featured on page 96. It would be wisest to keep the leaves in their natural state rather than gild them, as randomly scattering them under the tablecloth could mean they may come into contact with food.

• Dress up the wine glasses for the party by tying gold ribbon bows around their stems. Make the loops and ends generous for a louche, relaxed look.

• Here's a clever way to combine napkin ties and place names. Source some tiny round gilded picture frames and write in the person's name (even better, put in their photo), and tie on using two ribbons—one to match the glass stem ribbons and a wider gold chiffon. Cut the ribbons to the same length, lay the narrow ribbon over the wider one, then tie them together onto the frame.

• Make a sparkly table center by filling a large stemmed glass bowl with gold, silver, and metallic balls. Try piling the sequin balls from page 72 on top of the display.

golden crowns

Treat your guests like royalty by placing a crown at every setting. Jewel-encrusted and "ermine" trimmed, their cute, flirty style promises not to spoil any ladies' hairstyles; yet they look fun perched on a thinning pate too! Lined up down the table, they also play a major part in the tablescape. Either make them all the same, as here, or create ladies' and gentlemen's versions, ringing the changes with the colors or beading. You could also write names on the crowns so they double up as place cards.

Materials

To make 5 crowns

- Template materials (see p. 120)
- Approx 16 × 23in (42 × 59cm/A2 size) sheet of gold card
- Glue stick
- Approx 16 × 23in (42 × 59cm/A2 size) sheet of gold giftwrap
- Stapler
- Beading needle
- Gold sewing thread
- 45 gold ¹⁄₂in (1cm) sequins
- 45 pink ¹⁄₂in (1cm) sequins
- 45 blue ¹⁄₄in (5mm) glass beads
- 90 tiny gold beads
- 3yd (2.7m) elasticated gold cord
- Fabric adhesive
- 60in (1.75m) cream downy trim

1 Enlarge and cut out the template on page 126. Use this to cut five crown shapes out of the gold card. Glue these onto the reverse side of the giftwrap, then cut them out. Form the crowns with the gold card on the inside, then staple the two edges together to fix in position.

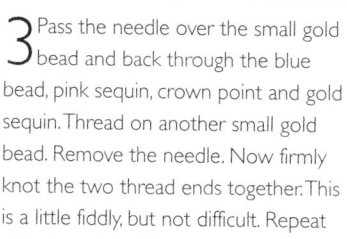

2 Using the beading needle, attach gold thread through the eye, then thread on one gold sequin. Working from the inside of the crown, pass the needle through one of the crown points. Thread on one pink sequin, one blue bead, and one tiny gold bead.

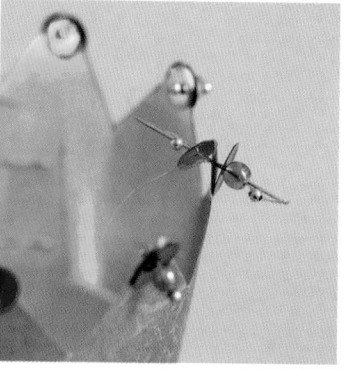

3 Pass the needle over the small gold bead and back through the blue bead, pink sequin, crown point and gold sequin. Thread on another small gold bead. Remove the needle. Now firmly knot the two thread ends together. This is a little fiddly, but not difficult. Repeat with the other eight points.

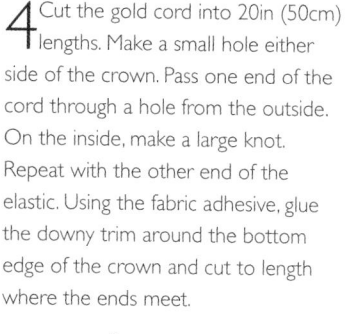

4 Cut the gold cord into 20in (50cm) lengths. Make a small hole either side of the crown. Pass one end of the cord through a hole from the outside. On the inside, make a large knot. Repeat with the other end of the elastic. Using the fabric adhesive, glue the downy trim around the bottom edge of the crown and cut to length where the ends meet.

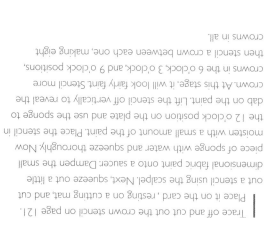

King's crown plates

No need to rush out and buy special Christmas plates when you can adapt your regular plain ones. These have been decorated around the rim with sequin-adorned sparkly crowns, whilst gold-rubbed skeleton leaves lend interest to the center, held in position by delightful glass top plates. It's a pretty trick that can be copied with different motifs and materials for celebrations throughout the year. The glass plates not only offer endless scope for customizing the crockery, they also provide an important health role, as food is kept well clear of any possible toxins.

Materials

For each plate

- Template materials (see p. 120)
- Small piece of card
- Scalpel and cutting mat
- Gold metallic three-dimensional fabric paint
- Saucer
- Small piece of sponge
- I white dinner plate
- Tube glitter glue in gold
- 32 small gold sequins
- I skeletonized magnolia leaf
- Picture framer's gold rub
- I glass plate

Trace off and cut out the crown stencil on page 121. Place it on the card , resting on a cutting mat, and cut out a stencil using the scalpel. Next, squeeze out a little dimensional fabric paint onto a saucer. Dampen the small piece of sponge with water and squeeze thoroughly. Now moisten with a small amount of the paint. Place the stencil in the 12 o'clock position on the plate and use the sponge to dab on the paint. Lift the stencil off vertically to reveal the crown. At this stage, it will look fairly faint. Stencil more crowns in the 6 o'clock, 3 o'clock and 9 o'clock positions, then stencil a crown between each one, making eight crowns in all.

Crowns around the plate rims, applied using fabric paint and children's glitter glue, make charming decoration that can easily be washed off. The gold-rubbed skeletonized leaves, placed beneath clear glass plates, bring dramatic interest to the table.

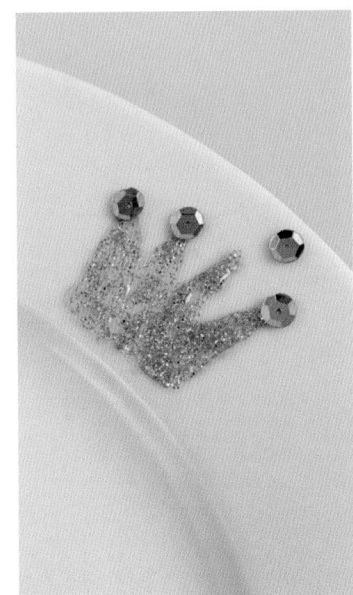

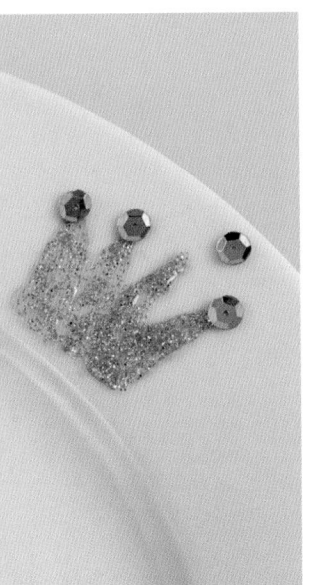

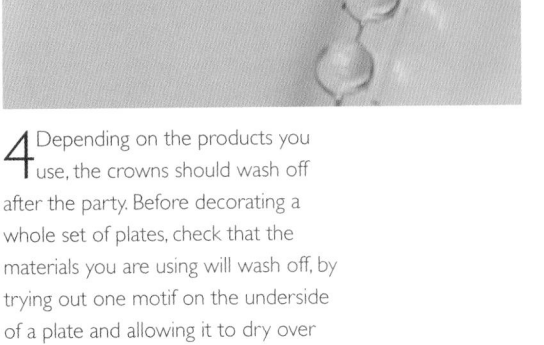

2 Repeat with all the other plates. Allow the paint to dry before going on to the next stage. Now go over each of the crowns on one plate using the glitter glue. They will now look much stronger.

3 Before the glue dries, stick a gold sequin onto each crown point. To ensure they stick, at this stage, complete one plate before going on to the next. When the crowns are complete, you can clean up the edges by gently scraping off any extraneous paint using the scalpel.

4 Depending on the products you use, the crowns should wash off after the party. Before decorating a whole set of plates, check that the materials you are using will wash off, by trying out one motif on the underside of a plate and allowing it to dry over two days before cleaning it off.

5 Skeletonized magnolia leaves are usually available from florists and their suppliers. However, at Christmas time, especially if there has been a frost and/or snow, you could find many naturally skeletonized fallen leaves outside. Put picture framer's gold rub onto one leaf for each plate. Allow to dry overnight.

6 Once the skeletonized leaves are completely dry, place them in the center of the white plates. Next, take the glass plates and place them over the leaves to fix them into position.

Christmas giving

The joy of Christmas lies in the giving, and the old adage of "it's the thought that counts" rings true every time. It's very often the smaller gifts, handmade and wrapped with love, that mean the most, and this is where all members of the family can join in, whatever their age. Consumable gifts are usually the most gratefully received by all ages, so cook some up in batches, then giftwrap with flair for friends, neighbors, and family. Even small children love to mix and roll dough for cookies, ball up some truffles, or concoct peppermint creams—and it's a brilliant way of keeping them occupied in the over-excited run up to Christmas.

Christmas cookies

Christmas cookies make an enchanting gift. A simple recipe, a set of cookie cutters, some icing, and cake decorations are all you need to cook up delightful gifts for friends and family. They're so easy to make, and this is a great project that will get the children wanting to join in. Package them in cellophane bags with a pretty ribbon tie to take to your office to share with your workmates, or present a pile on a beautiful plate, which becomes the gift in itself for your neighbors.

1 Preheat the oven to 350°F (180°C/Gas 4). Line baking trays with baking parchment and grease with the butter wrapper.

2 In a large mixing bowl, mix up the butter, sugar, flour, baking powder, egg, and vanilla extract and form into a dough ball. Divide this into four and wrap in cling film, then refrigerate to keep cool.

3 Flour a wooden board and rolling pin and roll out the first piece of dough to a thickness of 1/4in (6mm). Cut out shapes using the cookie cutters and put on one of the baking trays. Re-roll the trimmings to cut more shapes. Repeat with the other pieces of dough.

4 Place the trays in a pre-heated oven for 6 minutes until the edges of the shapes are just beginning to turn golden. Allow the cookies to cool on their trays for a few minutes before transferring them to a cooling rack.

5 Sift the confectioner's sugar into a bowl and add just sufficient water to create a smooth, quite runny, icing when stirred. Divide the icing into three bowls and color each one with a different food coloring. Use the icing, writing icing, edible balls, and mini marshmallows to decorate the cookies.

Ingredients

- 1 cup (200g/8oz) butter
- ½ cup (100g/4oz) superfine (caster) sugar
- 3 cups (450g/15oz) all-purpose (plain) flour
- ½ tsp baking powder
- 1 extra-large (large UK) egg
- 1 tsp vanilla extract
- Confectioner's (icing) sugar
- Red, green, and yellow food coloring
- Pack of differently colored icing tubes for writing
- Metallic cake decorating balls
- Pack of mini marshmallows
- Plastic wrap

There are so many different ways to ice and present cookies. Look in stores during the run-up to Christmas and you are bound to find some cookie cutters in festive shapes. Alternatively, it is a simple enough process to cut the dough by hand before baking and packaging them. Even one or two in a bag make a delightful small gift. Here are some useful presentation ideas:

decorating ideas

ABOVE LEFT: Make stars special by icing in white, then using yellow writing icing to draw out a star shape on top. Pack them into cellophane bags, or wrap them up in gold tissue and tie with a gold metallic ribbon.

ABOVE CENTER: Ice Rudolph's body to match his nose, then wrap him up in frosty-looking wax wrap and tie up with a mini check red gingham ribbon.

ABOVE RIGHT: Give sheep a woolly look by icing in white then adding mini marshmallows (from cake decorating departments) for a fleece.

BELOW LEFT: A red heart iced into the center of the cookie can be sparkled up with silver cake decorating balls. Pick out the red with a simple red bow.

BELOW CENTER: Keep Christmas trees natural with a raffia tie, presented on a homespun checked napkin

BELOW RIGHT: The little angel looks gorgeous in her pink dress! Use writing icing tubes to give her curly blonde hair, dark eyes and red rosebud lips.

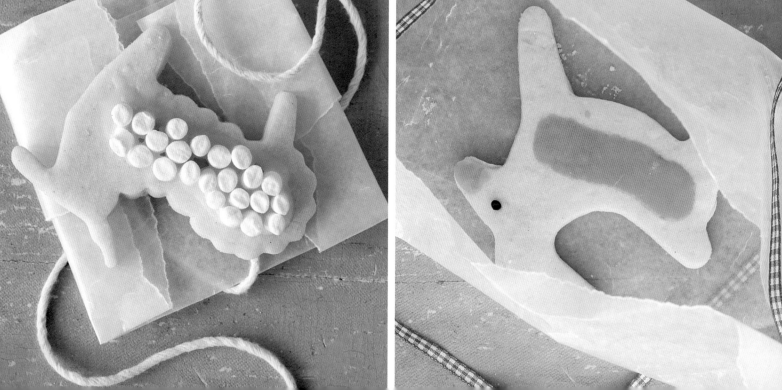

chocolate truffles

Undeniably indulgent, everyone adores chocolate truffles, so they make the perfect gift to make at home for people of all ages. Classic truffles are made with dark chocolate, and, when dusted with cocoa powder, resemble the highly prized culinary delicacy after which they are named. The chocolate variety are surprisingly easy to make, and once the method is mastered, you can make endless variations ranging from simply replacing dark chocolate with milk or white, to adding various flavorings, such as a splash of brandy or some orange zest.

1 Grate the chocolate and place in a bowl or pan set over a pan of boiling water so that it gently melts.

2 Pour the cream over the chocolate and gently whisk it to combine, to make a ganache. Add the vanilla extract.

3 Cover the bowl with plastic wrap and allow the ganache to cool to room temperature, then refrigerate for two hours until it is a suitable consistency for rolling.

4 Roll the ganache into small bite-size balls and dust with sifted cocoa powder. Place on a tray covered with wax paper or cling film to set. The truffles can be kept in a box in the refrigerator for up to a week. Place in mini foil cases to serve.

Ingredients

- 8oz (200g) dark chocolate
- $^{2}/_{3}$ cup (160ml) double (heavy) cream
- 1 tsp vanilla extract
- Unsweetened cocoa powder

*variations:

Truffles can be rolled in chocolate vermicelli, chopped nuts, desiccated coconut, or other cake-making decorations, or rolled in melted chocolate to give a different "bite." Truffles for adults can be flavored with alcohol. Choose strong flavors that will not be overwhelmed by the rich chocolate, such as brandy, rum, or Calvados.

peppermint creams

Pretty and snow-like, peppermint creams are a favorite Christmas confection, providing a fresh contrast to all the traditional rich food. A popular choice with children and adults alike, these treats are so easy to make, so why not get the kids to help you? They'll love cutting them into shapes, or place confectioners' decorations on them. Make several batches and add a few drops of coloring to some, for a sugar-almond-shade collection. Peppermint creams in white and blue make delightful after-dinner treats. Piled onto a pretty glass cake stand, peppermint creams—both decorated and parceled up—make a charming table center.

Ingredients
- 1 egg white
- 2⅓ cups (450g/1lb) confectioner's (icing) sugar
- 3–4 drops of peppermint extract
- Blue food coloring

1 Beat the egg white until it is frothy but not stiff. Sift the confectioner's sugar and add enough to the egg white to make a fairly stiff, kneadable mixture. Add the peppermint extract. If desired, split the mixture in two, and add food coloring to make treats in different colors.

2 Dust a surface with confectioner's sugar and knead the mixture to a firm paste. Roll into small balls and flatten, or cut into shapes.

3 Place the shapes onto parchment, waxed, or silicon paper, then add some confectioners' decorations, before leaving in a cool place for 24 hours to dry out. Once solid, wrap them in paper and finish with a pretty piece of ric rac or a gingham ribbon. Store the finished treats in an airtight container.

NB The raw egg white in this recipe means it is not suitable for ill or elderly people, women who are pregnant or breastfeeding, young children, and babies.

Cutout cards

Make special cards for your nearest and dearest by cutting out shapes from ordinary copy paper, then mounting them onto pretty colored card. Papercut collages have their traditions rooted in Europe, going back hundreds of years, and were made for many festivals, including Christmas and Easter. The simplest are cut out using embroidery scissors, though traditionally, more complicated designs included lattice work and designs within designs, which required the use of a scalpel. These four modern designs have lost none of the charm of the originals: indeed, their simple shapes, smooth lines and sugar-almond shades, lend added appeal.

dove collage card

A symbol of peace, this delightful dove brings a universal message. His clean, smooth lines not only give him modern appeal, but are also very easy to cut. Once you've completed one, you'll soon find you get quicker and could make cards for all your closest loved ones. Mount the cutouts in layers on different colored cards to bring greater depth. Even the narrow fillet of blue between two green layers serves to set off the dove better, giving the whole card a special quality that the recipients will no doubt treasure.

Materials

- Template materials (see p. 120)
- I sheet US Letter (A4) paper
- Tracing paper
- Scalpel and cutting mat and/ or embroidery scissors
- Steel rule
- I sheet US Ledger (A3) green card
- I sheet US Ledger (A3) blue card
- Glue stick

I Trace off the templates on page 123, separate the different elements, and place them on the sheet of copy paper, on top of a cutting mat. Then, using scissors or scalpel, cut around the outlines. The detail cuts on the wings and corner pieces will have to be cut using a scalpel.

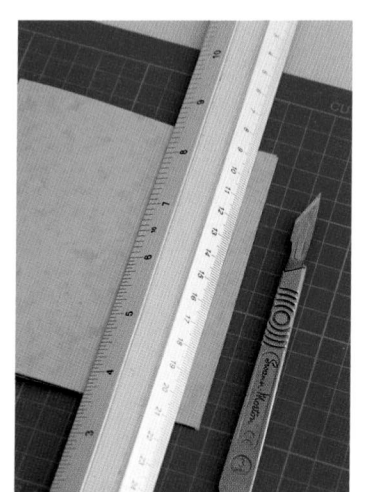

2 Using the scalpel, cutting mat and steel rule, cut one piece of green card measuring 3¾ x 3¾in (10 x 10cm) square and another measuring 8½ x 4¾in (24 x 12cm). Also cut a piece of blue card measuring 4¼ x 4¼in (11 x 11cm)

3 Arrange the cutouts on the small piece of green card and, once you're happy with the arrangement, stick the pieces in position.

4 Next, lightly score the rectangular piece of card at the halfway fold mark and fold. Glue the blue square centrally over this, ensuring the fold is on the left-hand side. Finally, glue the decorated green square centrally over the blue square.

giftwrap ideas

The very special gifts you buy for
your loved ones deserve special
attention. Let them stand out in the
crowd of parcels, announcing their
status and the love with which they
are given. You don't have to go out
and buy special Christmas paper—
you can choose a basic, then add all
sorts of bits and pieces to make
them special. Brown parcel wrap
always looks good, as does crisp
plain white, or tissue of any color
you like. This is not only cost
effective, but it will mean the parcels
all look good together, whatever
the age or gender of the recipient!
These parcels have all been
wrapped in inexpensive gold tissue
and labeled with ordinary brown
luggage labels, then dressed up with
string, ribbons, braids, leaves, and
cut-out paper to create four very
different looks.

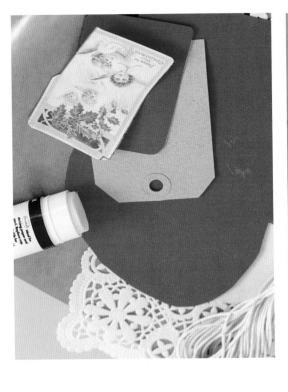

have a heart

Hearts make a wonderful icon at any time of the year. Although in many countries it is more usually associated with Valentine's Day, in Denmark and Germany it is a popular Christmas motif, and here it has been made all the more Christmasy, set against the gold tissue paper.

idea

A rectangular paper doily laid over the top of the parcel makes a charming feminine background for a huge red heart cut from card. The luggage label follows the theme when layered with a smaller red rectangle and Victorian motif cut from an old Christmas card. It's all tied up with fine string tied in a bow, adding detail, yet not distracting from the overall design.

filigree gold

The delightful translucent layers of this parcel give it all the charm of a Christmas ball gown. Gold tissue paper again provides the base, this time topped by a large, gilded skeletonized leaf. A smaller leaf, layered over the luggage label, echoes the translucency of the parcel. All tied up with gold ribbon, it's almost a shame that it has to be destroyed to reveal the gift inside.

idea

A tube of picture framer's metallic rub is the key to this look. The luggage label and both leaves have been given the Midas touch before being tied up with the gold ribbon.

natural solution

Evergreens are a great source of robust leaves that will stay looking fresh for days, providing excellent, inexpensive materials for decorating giftwrap. These are variegated holly leaves (from the top of the tree, so they don't have spikes), but laurel and bay are very similar.

idea

Here, the luggage label has been given a fresh look by cutting the end in curves to a point, then rubbing on gold as on page 117. The leaves have also been rubbed with gold to tone with the parcel. It's all tied up with a pretty braid in gold and red.

in the red

This tempting parcel has been layered up with gold tissue, a strip of handmade white paper, and then a strip of inexpensive red giftwrap, from which the hearts were also cut. Red-and-white striped ribbon ties it all together for a bold, modern look.

idea

Layers always look impressive, and although these papers are all inexpensive, you can make a parcel look exotic by using strips of more expensive paper or even fabric in a similar way. Coordinate the luggage label by layering it up in the same way, possibly adding interesting motifs cut from another paper.

Christmas Bunting page 26

You will need tracing paper, a pencil, and scissors to create these templates.

templates

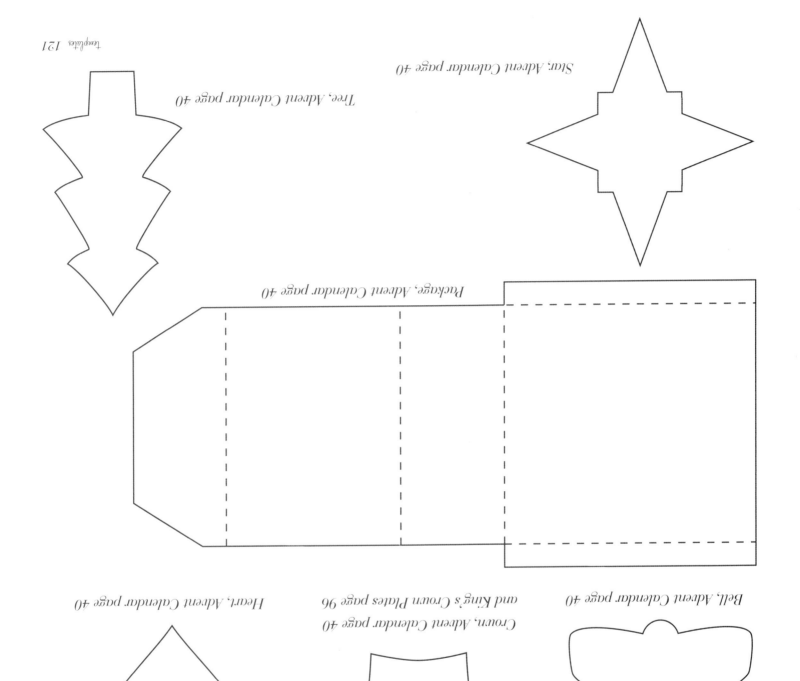

Tree, Advent Calendar page 40

Star, Advent Calendar page 40

Package, Advent Calendar page 40

Heart, Advent Calendar page 40

Crown, Advent Calendar page 40 and King's Crown Plates page 96

Bell, Advent Calendar page 40

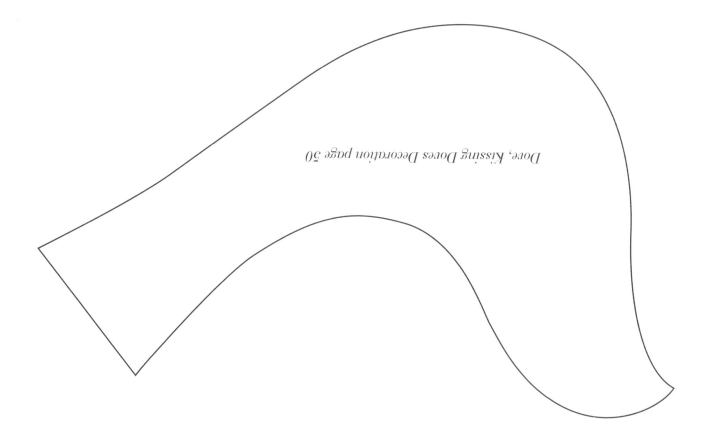

Dove, Kissing Doves Decoration page 50

Wing, Kissing Doves Decoration page 50

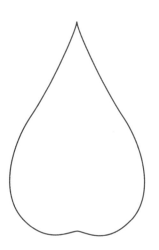

Heart, Kissing Doves Decoration page 50

Victorian Christmas Shoe
page 52
Enlarge to twice this size

Use this line as
the base of the
Boot template

Use this line as the top
of the Shoe template

Victorian Christmas Stocking Boot
page 52
Enlarge to twice this size

Victorian Christmas Stocking Cuff
page 52
Enlarge to twice this size

Dove Cottage Card page 112

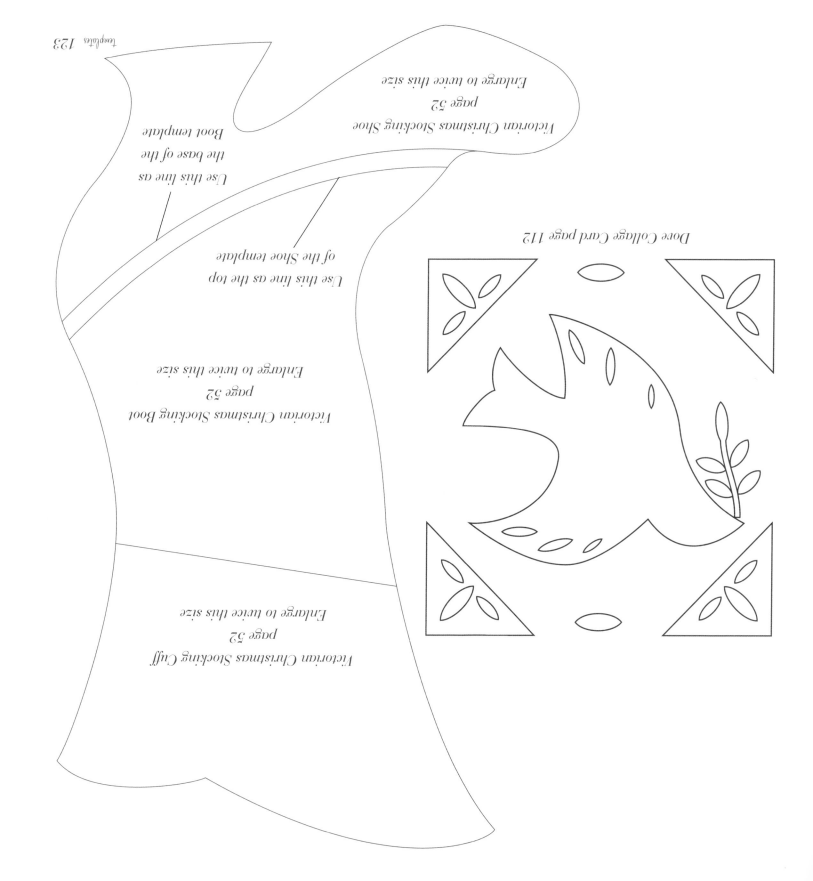

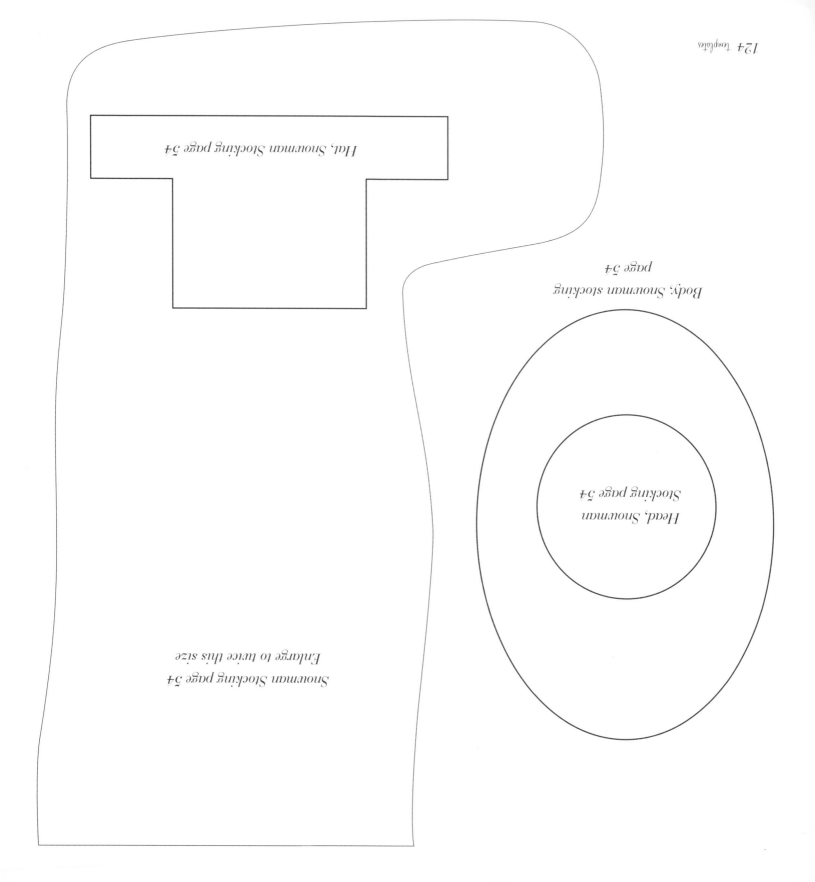

Hat, Snowman Stocking page 54

Body, Snowman stocking
page 54

Head, Snowman
Stocking page 54

Enlarge to twice this size

Snowman Stocking page 54

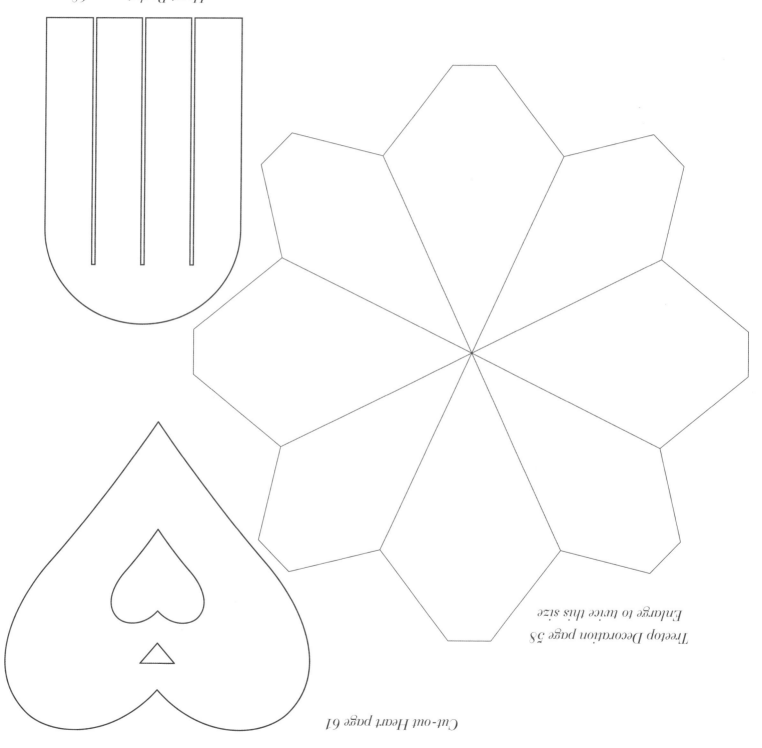

Heart Baskets page 68

Treetop Decoration page 55
Enlarge to twice this size

Cut-out Heart page 61

Golden Crowns page 94
Enlarge to twice this size

Jingle Bells Table place name page 80

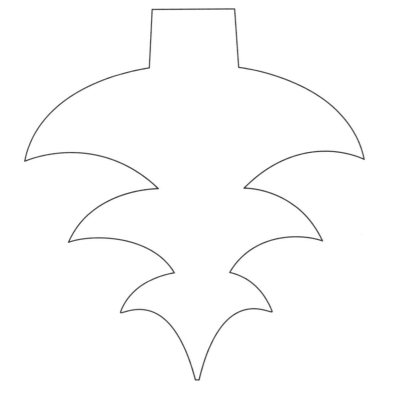

Ears, Knitted Tree Pets page 74

Antlers, Knitted Tree Pets page 74

Suppliers

North America

Amy Butler
For stockists see
www.amybutlerdesigns.com

Art Supplies Online
800-967-7367
www.artsuppliesonline.com

Crafts etc.
800-888-0321
www.craftsetc.com

Craft Site Directory
Useful online resource
www.craftsitedirectory.com

Create For Less
866-333-4463
www.createforless.com

Cia's Palette
4155 Grand Ave S.
Minneapolis MN 55409
612-229-5227
www.ciaspalette.com

Hobby Lobby
Stores nationwide
www.hobbylobby.com

Jo-ann Fabric & Crafts
Stores nationwide
www.joann.com

Michaels
Stores nationwide
www.michaels.com

Panduro Hobby
Online craft supplies
www.pandurohobby.com

Purl Patchwork
147 Sullivan Street
New York NY 10012
212-420-8798
www.purlsoho.com

Reprodepot Fabrics
413-527-4047
www.reprodepotfabrics.com

S&S Worldwide Craft Supplies
800-288-9941
www.ssww.com

Sunshine Crafts
800-729-2878
www.sunshinecrafts.com

Z and S Fabrics
681 S. Muddy Creek Road
Denver PA 17157
717-336-4028
www.zandsfabrics.com

UK

Beadworks Online Bead Store
www.beadworks.co.uk

The Button Queen
19 Marylebone Lane
London W1V 2NF
020 7935 1505
www.thebuttonqueen.co.uk

The Cloth House
47 Berwick Street
London W1F 8SJ
020 7437 5155
www.clothhouse.co.uk

Creative Beadcraft
20 Beak Street
London W1F 9RE
020 7629 9964
www.creativebeadcraft.co.uk

Fred Aldous Online Craft Materials
www.fredaldous.co.uk

John Lewis
Stores nationwide
www.johnlewis.com

La Belle Fleur
22B Bellevue Road
London SW17 7EB
www.labellefleur.com

La Cuisinere
81–83 Northcote Road
London SW11 6PJ
www.la-cuisiniere.co.uk

Lakeland Creative Kitchenware Online
www.lakeland.co.uk

Liberty
Great Marlborough Street
London W1B 5AH
020 7743 1234
www.liberty.co.uk

London Bead Shop
24 Earlham Street
London WC2H 9LN
020 7379 9214
www.londonbeadshop.co.uk

Paperchase
Stores nationwide
www.paperchase.co.uk

VV Rouleaux
102 Marylebone Lane
London W1V 2QD
020 7224 5179
www.vvrouleaux.com

Wimbledon Sewing Machine Shop
292–312 Balham High Road
London SW17 7AA
www.craftysewer.com

Acknowledgments

I'd like to say a huge thank you to everyone involved in the production of this book. As it would not be what it is without any one of them, to save any preferential treatment, in order of appearance, here goes…
To Cindy Richards who conceived the idea in the first place and encouraged me with imaginative titbits bought from far and wide; Caroline Arber, whose photographs so exquisitely capture the spirit of Christmas and for her unstinting work, far beyond the call of duty; Sally Powell and Gillian Haslam for their enthusiasm; Pete Jorgensen for his dedication, clear headedness, good humor, and patience; Luis Peral-Aranda for his wonderful, imaginative designs produced to vicious deadlines.
And last, but not least, to my family: Richard, Zoe, and Faye for their inspiration over past Christmases and support over this.

Contributors

Joan Cordoza at La Belle Fleur—Pine and Cinnamon Wreath, Stair Garland and Mantel Garland
Faye Harrison—Peppermint Creams and Chocolate Truffles
Rosa Roberts—Cutout Cards and Cross-stitch Cushion design